LEADING THE EVOLUTION

How to Make Personalized Competency-Based Education a Reality

MIKE RUYLE

with

Tamera Weir O'Neill • Jeanie M. Iberlin • Michael D. Evans • Rebecca Midles

MARZANO Resources

555 North Morton Street
Bloomington, IN 47404
888.849.0851
FAX: 866.801.1477

email: info@MarzanoResources.com
MarzanoResources.com

Printed in the United States of America

Library of Congress Control Number: 2018938203

ISBN: 978-1-943360-22-2

FSC
www.fsc.org
MIX
Paper from responsible sources
FSC® C011935

Editorial Director: Sarah Payne-Mills
Art Director: Rian Anderson
Managing Production Editor: Kendra Slayton
Senior Production Editor: Tara Perkins
Senior Editor: Amy Rubenstein
Copy Editor: Evie Madsen
Proofreader: Jessi Finn
Text and Cover Designer: Abigail Bowen

Portions of this text also appear in Mike Ruyle's doctoral dissertation (Ruyle, 2014).

ACKNOWLEDGMENTS

The continued evolution of traditional educational paradigms is challenging yet critical work. We would like to acknowledge some of the leaders in the field who made this book possible: Libby Child, Travis Anderson, Cale VanVelkinburgh, Wayne Hoy, Robert Marzano, Alec Ross, Tim Waters, Ray McNulty, Richard DeLorenzo, Virgel Hammonds, Marilyn King, Kirk Miller, Ken Gibson, Will Dickerson, Jen Algard, John Gallagher, Chuck Schwahn, Bea McGarvey, Ginger Blackmon, Jayne Downey, Art Bangert, Brian Farragher, Robert Macy, and Shawna Rader-Kelly.

Marzano Resources would like to thank the following reviewers:

Steven Ast
Principal
Brecksville-Broadview Heights High School
Broadview Heights, Ohio

Jennifer Galindo
Principal
Grassy Waters Elementary School
West Palm Beach, Florida

Rachel Jones
Principal
T. C. Gurney Elementary School
Chagrin Falls, Ohio

Paul M. Lucas
Principal
Orange High School
Pepper Pike, Ohio

Tammy Milligan
Principal
Lincoln Elementary School
Lindsay, California

Susan Pegram
Principal
Lost Lake Elementary School
Clermont, Florida

Tori Stephens-Shauger
Co-Founder, Executive Director, and Principal
ACE Leadership High School
Albuquerque, New Mexico

TABLE OF CONTENTS

CHAPTER 2

CHAPTER 3

ABOUT THE AUTHORS

Mike Ruyle, EdD, served as a teacher, athletic coach, and school leader in the San Francisco Bay Area and Bozeman, Montana. He led the creation and implementation of the first fully functional, performance-based school in Montana and is a recognized authority in the areas of social justice, educational equity, mindfulness, and trauma-informed care in schools. His leadership experience in personalized competency-based education has made him a sought-after national and international presenter for numerous schools, districts, state agencies, and conferences.

Mike earned bachelor of arts degrees in history and English from the University of San Francisco, as well as master's and doctoral degrees in educational leadership from Montana State University. To learn more about Mike's work, follow @MikeRuyle on Twitter.

Tamera Weir O'Neill, MS, is an assistant principal in Bozeman, Montana, and has previously served as an English teacher, instructional coach, and curriculum specialist. In addition to twenty years of classroom experience, Tamera also has extensive experience as a teacher leader in developing a personalized, competency-based model of education in an alternative school setting as well as expanding the system into the general setting. Her professional commitment is to promote the design and implementation of educational systems that customize learning experiences for every student.

Tamera holds a bachelor of arts degree in English from Montana State University and a master of science degree in curriculum and instruction from Western Governors University.

Jeanie M. Iberlin, EdD, has thirty-three years of experience in the educational realm. She served twenty-one years as an administrator and has been honored as the Wyoming Assistant Superintendent of the Year for her leadership in the areas of formative assessment and standards-based grading, curriculum, and instruction. She also has extensive experience as a middle school principal and high school English teacher. Jeanie is an associate and professional development trainer for Marzano Resources, leading administrators, instructional facilitators, teachers, and other staff members in dynamic presentations of curriculum, instruction, assessment, evaluation, and professional development. She is the author of *Cultivating Mindfulness in the Classroom.*

She earned an undergraduate degree in education from Chadron State College, a master's degree from the University of Wyoming, and a doctoral degree in education administration from Montana State University.

Michael D. Evans, EdD, serves as the assistant superintendent for curriculum and instruction for Monett R-1 School District in Monett, Missouri. He has more than twenty years of experience as a classroom teacher, school counselor, building-level leader, and district-level leader. Michael helped lead the transition to standards-based learning from the district level and has been a regular presenter at state leadership conferences.

He holds a bachelor's degree in education from Missouri Southern State University, a master of science degree in counseling from Missouri State University, an education specialist degree in educational administration from William Woods University, and a doctoral degree in educational leadership from Lindenwood University. To learn more about Michael's work, visit www.linkedin.com/in/michaeldevans71 and http://schoolbymike.com or follow @michaeldevans71 on Twitter.

Rebecca Midles is the executive director of performance-based systems at Mesa County Valley School District 51 in Grand Junction, Colorado. She has more than eighteen years of experience in the field of competency-based learning, serving in the roles of teacher, site administrator, board member, district administrator, consultant, and parent. Rebecca started her work in Alaska and then continued to work with competency-based school districts all over the United States. She was the performance-based learning specialist at Lindsay Unified School District in California. Rebecca is dedicated to her vision that learners become leaders by developing a strong sense of self and the ability to advocate for their pursuits. She believes her role is to build and support systems that propel and enable the important work of student empowerment. To learn more about Rebecca's work, follow @akrebecca on Twitter.

To book Mike Ruyle, Tamera Weir O'Neill, Jeanie M. Iberlin, Michael D. Evans, or Rebecca Midles for professional development, contact pd@SolutionTree.com.

INTRODUCTION

The significant problems of our time cannot be solved by the same level of thinking that created them.

—Albert Einstein

The young people of the 21st century face a future far more uncertain than at any other time in recent memory. Journalist and author Thomas L. Friedman (2016) referred to this era as the *age of accelerations* and pointed at two of the planet's largest forces—(1) technology and (2) globalization—as primarily driving the tectonic movements shaping the contemporary world. Indeed, the advent of modern technology has increased the speed with which any person can gain access to information and knowledge. National shifts away from industrialized economic systems to those of digital, global economies epitomize the impact, which has resulted in massive foundational changes to the societal landscape. Author, speaker, and international advisor on education Sir Ken Robinson (2001) stated, "There are forces at work now for which there are no precedents" (p. 5). He continued by declaring, "New technologies are revolutionizing the nature of work everywhere. . . . What is certain is that in the next 50 to 100 years, our children will need to confront challenges that are unique in human history" (Robinson, 2001, p. 6).

An upshot of this phenomenon is, in the coming years, a high percentage of 21st century students will compete for jobs yet to be created, and the skills necessary to perform in those new roles are constantly evolving. In his book *The Industries of the Future*, innovation policy expert Alec Ross (2016) made the point that although technology will continue to inject tremendous energy and opportunity into the labor market, automated structures will also replace people in a vast array of jobs. The new technologies can allow for tremendous improvement in the human condition, but only so long as people "create the systems to adapt their workforces, economies, and societies to the inevitable disruption" that is inherent in periods of dramatic growth and change (Ross, 2016, p. 37).

Stagnant Systems in a Changing World

As the world continues to advance at such relentless, breakneck speed, schools are under increasingly intense pressure to develop just as quickly to prepare all students to succeed and thrive in this uncertain future. But the reality is the traditional model of K–12 education is ill-equipped to operate in the complex, rapid-fire world of tomorrow. This is not a new assertion. In 2005, author Daniel H. Pink predicted the American job market would shift dramatically when he said, "Outsourcing is overhyped in the near term. But it's underhyped in the long term" (p. 39). In 2011, organizational psychologist Wyatt Warner Burke stated that American schools are being forced to play catch-up with the rest of the world's advanced nations due to an inability to effectively change their educational paradigm. And in 2016, Ross asserted emerging nations in Asia and Eastern Europe are placing a premium on educating students to excel in industries that will drive the future global marketplace. Thus, the increasing technological and innovative capacity of these countries is creating a skills gap in which many young learners will be "globalized and automated out of jobs" (Ross, 2016, p. 34). A number of other experts have reinforced this specific declaration. For example, in a widely noted study, Carl Benedikt Frey and Michael A. Osborne (2013) examined the probable impact of potential automation on 702 occupations and reported that 47 percent of workers in the United States held jobs with a high risk for obsolescence. They concluded that continued improvements in machine learning would have an even stronger impact across a wide range of occupations in the future. In 2015, Georg Graetz and Guy Michaels published the results of their research gathered from 1993 to 2007 in the United States as well as sixteen other countries and presented evidence that industrial automation has crowded out low-skilled and, to a lesser extent, middle-skilled workers. Specifically, they warned that most workers in transportation and logistics industries (including taxi and delivery drivers), office support fields (including receptionists and security guards), and sales and services positions (such as cashiers, counter clerks, telemarketers, and accountants) are likely to be replaced by computerization. And Jerry Kaplan (2015), author of *Humans Need Not Apply*, predicted upheaval in the labor market that would have equal impact on both the blue- and white-collar sectors.

Simply put, the time-based educational structure educators have inherited and maintained from the Industrial Age no longer fits the needs of learners, communities, or innovative industries. The traditional, industrialized model of compulsory schooling was created more than 150 years ago and quickly morphed into a system that would sort and select which students would be prepared for opportunities in higher education and which students would move into the military or workforce jobs that didn't necessarily require innovation, critical thinking, or creative problem solving. In 2000, educational scholar Diane Ravitch made the point that many of the staid examples of the antiquated industrialized system, including traditional master schedules, the A–F grading system, and agrarian-based school calendars, have remained relatively unchanged for over a century (Anderson, 2014). Furthermore, as education consultants Fred Bramante and Rose Colby (2012) pointed out:

> *The primary problem with public education in America is that the foundational structure, in which time is a constant and achievement is a variable, is a fatal flaw that will doom our system of public education to endless mediocrity, regardless of how much money we pour into it. And that mediocrity will translate into failure for our country to produce the educated citizenry necessary to achieve the economic goal of yet another American century. (p. 2)*

Since the National Commission on Excellence in Education's publication of *A Nation at Risk* in 1983, federal initiatives such as Goals 2000: Educate America Act, the Workforce Investment Act of 1998, the No Child Left Behind Act of 2001, Race to the Top, the Common Core State Standards, and the Every Student Succeeds Act have been implemented to address the need for schools to help improve individual student performance. Interestingly, data gleaned from the National Center for Education Statistics (Kena et al., 2014; McFarland et al., 2017) clearly illustrate the reality that measured reading and mathematics achievement scores in the United States have not significantly improved since the early 1970s.

In response to this stagnation, the U.S. government has distributed billions of dollars to schools, and there have been loud, public calls for the increased accountability of all educators. In addition, the myriad of government-mandated initiatives has inflicted intense pressure on the education system and corresponding profound daily impact on people operating in schools. For example, federal, state, and local content-area standards have placed increasingly oppressive and unrealistic expectations on teachers by demanding they cram years of content into 180 school days (Marzano, Yanoski, Hoegh, & Simms, 2013), fueling the burnout and turnover that are readily apparent within the ranks of teachers across the United States (Cohen & Janicki-Deverts, 2012; Ingersoll & May, 2016; Kyriacou, 1987). Although educators at all levels are seemingly unanimous in their assertion that teachers are working harder than ever and are committed to helping learners experience success by virtually every measure (and despite a vast array of initiatives), overall student achievement has not changed appreciably (Kena et al., 2014; McFarland et al., 2017). Furthermore, Ethan Yazzie-Mintz (2010), former project director of *Charting the Path From Engagement to Achievement: A Report on the 2009 High School Survey of Student Engagement*, highlighted how K–12 student engagement data continue to exhibit exceedingly troubling trends:

> *Kids are bored, not connected to school. We've got similar numbers in terms of kids who are bored every day—about 49 percent of the kids are bored every day, 17 percent every class. That's two-thirds of the kids who are bored at least every day. (p. 4)*

These phenomena are not by-products of poor teacher effort, a lack of compelling research or resources, or a disinterested public, but rather due to the fact that the traditional model of schooling simply has not evolved to a more contemporary and relevant design. We would argue there are few, if any, successful businesses or organizations operating in the same way they did before the 1970s. For example, if a doctor were to largely ignore specific medical advances that had become an accepted part of the research base and treat his or her patients with a protocol that was common prior to those advances, it would be called *malpractice*. Unfortunately, when this same thing happens in schools, it's called *tenure*. Bluntly stated, the traditional model of schooling is flawed and outdated in terms of meeting the needs of all learners in the modern world. And although there has been widespread, bipartisan political support to change the educational system (Kohn, 1999), we have witnessed consistent failure to effect substantive reform to the prevailing Industrial Age model (Fullan, 2007; Ravitch, 2000).

Traditional approaches to school reform typically focus on merely tweaking existing models. In other words, reformers often color inside the lines of the existing system. Essentially, this paradigm paralyzes schools, which are increasingly inadequate to the task at hand. Thus, 21st century educational leaders need to move away from a piecemeal approach to reform and embrace systemic growth—new thinking, new structures, and new strategies to move the system forward consistent with emerging realities in a digital, global society.

An Effective Model for Systemic Change

Specifically, there is a consensus forming that competency-based education systems—where students progress by demonstrating mastery of specified learning goals—may be the most viable way forward (Bloom, 1971; Bramante & Colby, 2012; Guskey, 2010; Hattie, 2009). In addition, personalized education also has a solid research base. Albert Bandura's (1977) work on the concept of *self-efficacy*, which refers to an individual's belief that he or she possesses the abilities to control his or her own life, has had a profound effect on education. In order to better tap into student self-efficacy, the research over subsequent decades has expanded to address the critical need to personalize the educational experience for the humans in a classroom by differentiating instructional strategies based on individual needs (Martin, 2011, 2012a; Martin & Liem, 2010; Pintrich, 2003; Schenck, 2011; Schunk, 2012). Ronald F. Ferguson (2015) redefined the concept of self-efficacy in learners as *student agency*, which he identifies as "the capacity and propensity to take purposeful initiative—the opposite of helplessness" (p. 1). Ferguson (2015) goes on to declare, "The development of agency may be as important an outcome of schooling as the skills we measure with standardized testing" (p. 1). This is the essence of personalized education.

Although the terms *personalized learning* and *competency-based learning* are not synonymous in the research, they are commonly referred to in the same light in the education field. In fact, the U.S. Department of Education (n.d.) offers a page on its website titled "Competency-Based Learning or Personalized Learning," using the terms in tandem to describe an instructional model that allows for students to progress through academic content via personalized learning opportunities and individualized pacing. Robert J. Marzano and his colleagues (2017) have acknowledged the intimate connection between the two constructs and, thus, coined the term *personalized competency-based education* (PCBE). We employ the same convention for the same purpose.

Evolving educational schemas systemwide to PCBE models will require a fundamental shift in how business is done in schools at all levels, from classroom teachers to building and district leaders to the college instructors conducting teacher preparation programs. This evolution also demands visionary people with strong skill sets to lead and manage schools to create and maintain substantive growth and positive changes in the future. This is the most difficult, yet critical, work educators do and the essence of true educational reform.

Leadership is a cooperative experience. As educational leadership specialists Viviane M. J. Robinson, Claire A. Lloyd, and Kenneth J. Rowe (2008) pointed out, "The more leaders focus their relationships, their work, and their learning on the core business of teaching and learning, the greater their influence on student outcomes" (p. 636). True evolution will only happen when school leaders are working alongside the teachers and students in the learning and implementation stages of a new paradigm. Leaders expect classroom teachers to build relationships with and foster growth in students. Thus, principals must build relationships with and foster growth in teachers by modeling what they want to see, striving to improve instructional skills, and cultivating and nurturing true lifelong learners. The traditional education system fails many students, but when 21st century educational leaders fully commit to the evolution of schools as an issue of social justice, they ensure educators will personalize education to meet the needs of *every* student.

Effectively increasing the overall academic capacity of all learners will not occur as a result of merely throwing a variety of instructional strategies at them in classrooms or tinkering with an outdated system. Many schools still focus on the same antiquated goals that protect the status quo, and across North America, governmental agencies' or education administrations' new initiatives have allowed—and even encouraged—schools to settle for tinkering with the Industrial Age system. It is clear, however, making minor changes within this educational model while rehashing the traditional pedagogy from a bygone era cannot address optimal student engagement, authentic learning, and sustained academic growth. Bramante and Colby (2012) highlighted the need to evolve to a system that allows for personalized student growth when they stated:

> *In order to truly engage each student, the system of education in the future must be built to address the needs of the whole child: the personal, social, physical, and academic needs of each student—not all students—each student. (p. 86)*

Such a transformational change in the fundamental nature of schooling will necessitate a paradigm shift in organization and structure.

A Framework for Implementation

Successful school evolution efforts rely heavily on a three-pronged leadership approach that actively involves not only the leader personally but also the leader's responsibility to cultivate optimistic teachers and engaged learners. In this book, the term for this three-pronged approach is the *evolutionary triad*. The triad (figure I.1) engages three equally important players in a school or district's educational evolution: (1) the transformational instructional leader, (2) the optimistic teacher, and (3) the engaged student. The evolutionary triad is a powerful concept that provides a framework for navigating change and growing capacity for action; it connects leadership, student engagement, and teacher optimism around PCBE within the overarching theme of social justice.

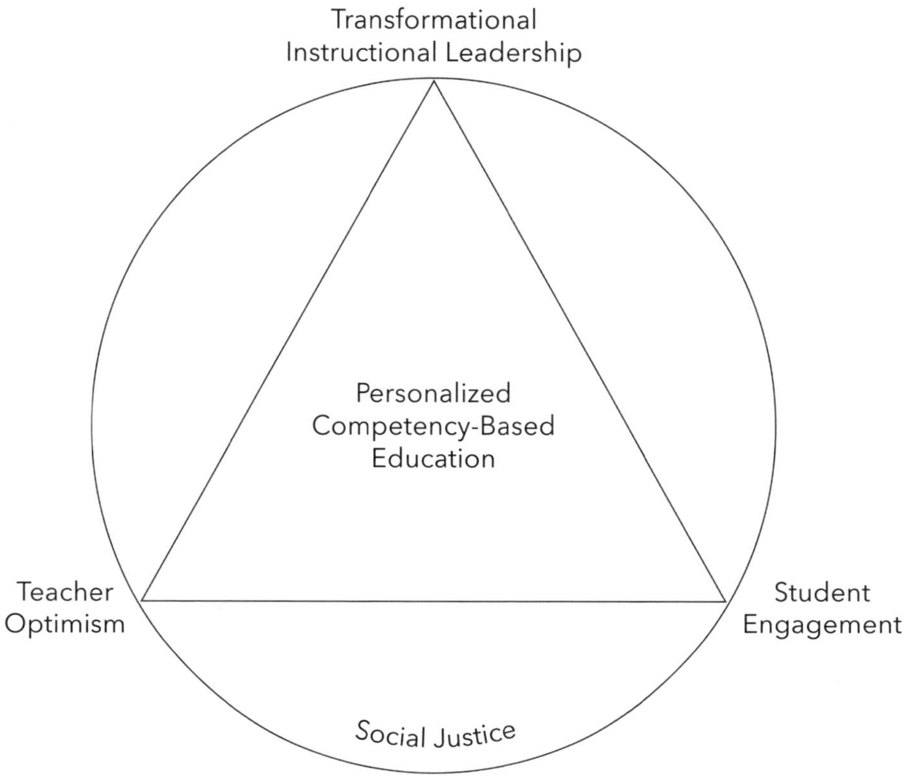

Source: Adapted from Anderson, 2014; Ruyle, 2014.

Figure I.1: The evolutionary triad.

This book, composed from the perspective of practitioners who have extensively studied and successfully implemented personalized competency-based education systems, presents fresh arguments for evolving the K–16 education system to a more contemporary and relevant model, emphasizing the leadership qualities and practices necessary to bring such a massive paradigm shift to fruition.

About This Book

This book will identify what next-generation schools look like and provide leaders with an overview of the behaviors that will facilitate the organizational and cultural shifts necessary to evolve existing educational paradigms. The single most important factor affecting student learning is the teacher (Marzano, 2018), and despite the system's constraints and limited time and resources, the vast majority of teachers do their absolute best. Nevertheless, it is imperative for school leaders and classroom teachers to actively adapt to an ever-changing world to continue serving the needs of children and communities. Educators need to continue working toward improving learning for every student without completely abandoning the public school system. In this sense, *evolve* is the strongest, most accurate, and most appropriate verb to use to describe this process because it alludes to the necessary growth of organisms and organizations to avoid extinction. *Evolution* is the word we will rely on continually throughout this book to describe this change process.

The book offers discussions and examples to bring the points of the evolutionary triad to life, and each point on the triad has an entire chapter devoted to its study. First, chapter 1 provides a foundation for understanding the PCBE model and the evolutionary triad, and why schools must utilize them to support educational evolution. Chapter 2 focuses on the top point in the triad, transformational instructional leadership, and presents the leadership mindsets and behaviors critical to implementation of the PCBE model. Chapter 3 deals specifically with the teacher element of the triad and addresses the construct of teacher optimism in detail. Chapter 4 examines the student engagement point of the triad and the unique role learners themselves have in bringing about evolutionary change in schools. Chapter 5 presents suggestions for how to sustain and improve once transformation has taken place.

Each chapter includes supporting research and theory, as well as clear direction and strategies for leaders to put the evolutionary triad into practice. In addition, you'll find feature quotes from stakeholders we and our colleagues have personally worked with since 2012, who speak to the real-life impacts of strong PCBE systems. The quotes presented verbatim herein come directly from research data via interviews—including those conducted for our own edification as well as those conducted jointly for author Mike Ruyle's (2014) and colleague Travis Anderson's (2014) doctoral dissertations—and personal conversations with leaders, teachers, and students in PCBE systems around the world, including those in North America, China, Central America, Canada, Australia, Singapore, and Finland.

CHAPTER 1

Foundations for Evolution

> *Today our very survival depends on our ability to stay awake, to adjust to new ideas, to remain vigilant, and to face the challenge of change.*
>
> —Martin Luther King Jr.

Part of the challenge of evolving educational systems is so many divergent stakeholder groups often claim to be education experts simply because they went to school. Another difficulty is that traditional schools operate under a familiar paradigm many people understand and accept. Physicist, historian, and philosopher Thomas S. Kuhn (1970) asserted that a paradigm maintains its enduring influence over a complex group of people because it represents the prevailing common sense as to how people have generally agreed to think and believe. Existing paradigms, however, can also limit one's ability to think outside the box or learn something new and innovative. People tend to stubbornly embrace their worldview and paradigms because they believe them to be true and to work.

Fortunately, however, when new information that is incompatible with the existing paradigm becomes apparent—when cognitive dissonance occurs—a new paradigm can often arise to take the place of the old system. This can be painful and difficult for people and organizations, so helping people see the failures of these paradigms and imagine new possibilities requires powerful, visionary leadership, moral courage, and a commitment to social justice. It is critical for 21st century educational leaders to drive a fundamental shift away from simply teaching curriculum and toward creating a culture of collective efficacy in which all school staff work collaboratively to improve student engagement and learning. In this chapter, we will first expand on the discussion we began in the introduction on the need to evolve schools, and then examine the PCBE model and the evolutionary triad in depth to investigate why

PCBE is the best approach for truly transforming traditional education paradigms and how the triad functions in supporting the implementation of this system.

The Need to Evolve Schools

Inequity notwithstanding, what we have done in schools has worked moderately well overall since the Industrial Revolution, and many educational systems have helped support a global standard of living that is higher than at any other point in history (Ross, 2016). But public education systems need to undergo a fundamental organizational shift to truly evolve schools and ensure their survival, effectiveness, and relevance. Teachers in the 21st century are trying to educate every learner—and ensure every student succeeds—in an anachronistic system never designed to achieve this goal. In fact, authors Charles Schwahn and Bea McGarvey (2012) pointed out the structures, procedures, and policies from the Industrial Age model actually *inhibit* educators' abilities to meet individual learner needs. This becomes clear when observing how the traditional school operates: a certain amount of expected work production in a fixed number of classes fits into a standard school year of roughly 180 days. Schools theoretically address a wide variety of learner aptitudes, interests, and abilities by accepting work in varying quality ranging from exceptional to average to failing. Finally, at the end of the specified time frame, virtually all students pass onto the next level based on their age and the same steps are repeated. Individual students are simply molded to the system, and the expected annual product is largely predetermined. This assembly-line model, however, is inconsistent with what works in learning and instruction, and impedes the capacity of teachers and schools to effectively apply the most powerful, contemporary educational research in classrooms (Schwahn & McGarvey, 2012). This palpable inconsistency results in stressors that impact students, teachers, and leaders and fails to effectively address educational equity and social justice.

For Students

There is overwhelming evidence that many young people do not feel prepared to take on the challenges that await them in college and careers (ACT, 2016). *TIME* magazine columnist Susanna Schrobsdorff (2016) referred to a broad spectrum of angst plaguing young people and cited data from the National Institute of Mental Health (NIMH; 2016) suggesting 30 percent of girls and 20 percent of boys experience anxiety that impairs their daily function. Related to this assertion, research from the American Academy of Pediatrics (Plemmons et al., 2018) reported that children ages 5 to 17 visited children's hospitals for suicidal thoughts or attempts at roughly twice the rate in 2015 as in 2008. And these hospital visits largely coincide with mid-winter and mid-spring academic terms.

While preK–12 schools are not necessarily the appropriate organizations to address all mental health issues, the benefit of empowering learners with strong skill sets, modeling positive interactions and solid self-concepts, and cultivating mindfulness along with emotional control is clear and undeniable, and could help avert problems later in life. If students are to be prepared for and successful in their adult lives, the scope of their education must expand beyond pure academic knowledge. High-quality education should develop these competencies by teaching students how to have compassion for themselves and others, manage and release stress, maintain focus, make healthy decisions, build relationships, and use effective strategies for handling their emotions (Iberlin, 2017).

Educators know intuitively, and the research is incontrovertible, that students learn at different rates and in different ways (Corbetta & Shulman, 2002; Meltzer, 2010; Semrud-Clikeman, 2007). Furthermore, since the 1990s, educators are much more advanced in terms of knowledge of the brain and learning and retention processes (R. Macy, personal communication, April 2018; Marzano & Marzano, 2015; Schenck, 2011). We have a much deeper understanding in terms of how motivation and perceived competence can impact individual student achievement (Anderson, 2014; Dweck, 1999, 2006; Martin, 2012a), and we know that teachers can provide high-quality feedback and targeted support through the use of valid formative assessment practice feedback (Anderson, 2014; Brookhart, 2008; Hattie, 2009; Marzano, 2012). Thus, instruction in schools should be tailored to address the individual needs of students, which provides the foundation from which to consider how to increase the overall quality of entire educational programs (Anderson, 2014; Cox, 2007).

"Lots of times, I go into a class and am excited, and the teacher turns me off to it forever. Required classes with a boring teacher make it totally not relevant for me."

—Ninth-grade student, Missouri

For Teachers

Although high school dropout and graduation rates have been a tremendous source of angst in education, another area not as well addressed publicly, yet of equally troubling concern, is teacher attrition rates due to burnout. University of Pennsylvania professor of education and sociology Richard M. Ingersoll and director of the Center for Research in Education and Social Policy at the University of Delaware Henry May (2016) asserted two main reasons teachers burn out and leave the profession: (1) lack of administrative support and (2) loss of autonomy corresponding to pressure to teach to the test. Authors Leib Sutcher, Linda Darling-Hammond, and Desiree Carver-Thomas (2016) found the U.S. teacher attrition rate hovers around 8 percent annually, and nearly 16 percent of teachers leave their schools every year. These rates are even higher in high-poverty schools, both urban and rural, as well as high-minority and low-performing schools, which further undermines student achievement due to teacher inexperience and faculty instability (Simon & Johnson, 2013). Among minority educators, over 15 percent of teachers leave their jobs annually (Ingersoll & May, 2016). In fact, whether transitioning out of teaching altogether or migrating from one school to another, minority teachers' careers have been less stable than those of nonminority teachers, which is especially true for male minority teachers, undermining efforts to address the lack of diversity in the field (Ingersoll & May, 2016).

This, ultimately, translates to less-experienced teachers replacing more than two hundred thousand educators who leave the profession every year (Sutcher et al., 2016). Part of this problem is tied directly to economic realities. In the United States, teachers still earn roughly 20–40 percent less than their similarly educated peers, and American teachers work longer hours than their counterparts from other countries (Allegretto & Mishel, 2016; Organisation for Economic Co-operation and Development, 2017; Strauss, 2017). But an equal part of the problem involves working conditions for teachers that include lack of resources, increased class sizes, increased numbers of students who come from challenging backgrounds (such as poverty or homelessness), and decreased autonomy due to government and district accountability mandates (Ingersoll, Merrill, & May, 2016a; Richmond, 2013).

Many of these data and much of this information are not new to the public. There is, indeed, a crisis of U.S. education, and this reality impacts every community on some level. As stated previously, U.S. achievement scores have been, at best, stagnant since at least the early 1970s (Kena et al., 2014; McFarland et al., 2017), and the call for increased accountability has produced pressure to teach more, teach faster, and teach louder. Add in the paperwork, supervisory responsibilities, and parent contacts, and it's understandable why teachers feel like they're running in quicksand rather than running a classroom. Teachers are tired. Top-down initiatives and constant pressure from a model that forces them to rush through academic content at the expense of authentic learning overwhelm teachers. The traditional, industrialized model of education places many teachers in an untenable situation in which success, measured in terms of high levels of growth for every student, is truly impossible.

"I taught for eleven years in traditional education and had decided to do something else just before I began working in the new model. I was so burned out and tired all the time. Teaching all these standards to all these kids and the pressure for success on some tests that don't really measure what they know is really ridiculous. I love working with kids, but life is too short to be pulling their teeth all the time. I was more excited about getting away from school than I ever was going into the school—everybody's like that—and it's just not right."

—*Middle school teacher, Vermont*

For Leaders

Teachers and students are not the only ones under a great deal of stress and anxiety; principals are suffering similarly. Through much of the 20th century, school principals were expected to serve as efficient mid-level managers, overseeing budgets, constructing master schedules, conducting faculty meetings, hiring staff, and delivering discipline. Although these responsibilities remain a building leader's burden to bear, these administrative functions are no longer a principal's only role. Twenty-first century building leaders must be both an effective manager and, more importantly, a leader of instruction.

In a longitudinal study of five hundred principals and one thousand educators that began in 2008, nearly half of principals revealed they were under "great stress several days a week" (MetLife, 2013, p. 5). Three-quarters shared that the job is too complex, and nearly half see the job as highly stressful. This stress is the greatest in middle and high schools (MetLife, 2013). Furthermore, principals' overall job satisfaction decreased from 68 percent to 59 percent from 2008 to 2013. Consequently, nearly one-third (32 percent) of school principals are likely to leave their career for a different occupation (MetLife, 2013). There are no easy answers to these stresses and dissatisfaction. The significant problems in the education system (leadership primarily entrenched in managerial duties, teachers isolated and powerless, and students disengaged and marginalized) will remain unless educators adopt new paradigms.

Highly effective principals are now tasked with challenging the traditional paradigms and creating a focus on increased student achievement (Hoy & Miskel, 2005) as well as ensuring their schools practice aspects of social justice (Larson & Barton, 2013; Noguera, 2003). Achieving these tasks depends on leaders creating a positive school culture that enables change to happen (Krüger, Witziers, & Sleegers, 2007; Muhammad, 2009). Thus, principal training must include aspects of innovative school systems as well as the pedagogy these new systems require (Turnbull, Riley, Arcaira, Anderson, & MacFarlane, 2013). True evolutionary change will only happen in schools when our leaders accept the mantle of not just instructional leadership but *transformational* instructional leadership and begin to focus on the individual learning needs of each student (Anderson, 2014). A principal must necessarily be an instructional leader in that he or she can mentor and guide the staff, but he or she also needs to take his or her practice to a higher level and assume the responsibility to *transform* his or her entire organization toward a new educational paradigm.

For Educational Equity and Social Justice

In 2009, U.S. secretary of education Arne Duncan said:

> *I believe that education is the civil rights issue of our generation. And if you care about promoting opportunity and reducing inequality, the classroom is the place to start. Great teaching is about so much more than education; it is a daily fight for social justice.*

South African anti-apartheid revolutionary, political leader, and philanthropist Nelson Mandela made an even more profound statement in 2003 when he said, "Education is the most powerful weapon we can use to change the world." In light of the tremendous changes in the world, education is truly the great human rights issue of our time. Yet, the traditional 20th century model of education is simply at odds with the requirements of a modern, global economy. Career and social success in a diverse, knowledge-based, 21st century economy depends on a strong, contemporary education, and by neglecting to cultivate the evolution of school structures, educators foster widespread inequality of opportunity. Thus, the urgency for schools to evolve toward a new organizational paradigm is clear; it is the key to promoting opportunity in a rapidly changing world and providing every student with the skills necessary to attain personal success and live the life he or she chooses. Educators need to reduce the opportunity gap.

According to Tom Vander Ark (2015), CEO of Getting Smart, an education consulting firm and leading advocate for innovations in learning, "There are now about 500 billionaires in the US, while more than one in four US kids live in poverty, a higher percentage of children than during the Great Recession" (p. 2). The link between poverty and the lack of educational opportunities is well chronicled and unequivocal (Heckman, 2011; Jerald & Ingersoll, 2002; National Institutes of Health, 2012). Students who do not graduate from high school earn substantially less in wages over a lifetime and may have far higher rates of incarceration and drug abuse than do their peers who do successfully navigate the educational system (Ratcliffe & McKernan, 2012; Sandstrom & Huerta, 2013).

In addition to teacher burnout and turnover, teacher shortages—particularly in the areas of mathematics, science, English as a second language, and special education—are especially alarming. The research of Sutcher et al. (2016) concluded half of all U.S. schools and 90 percent of high-poverty schools are struggling to find enough qualified special education teachers. Furthermore, students of color and those from high-poverty areas are less likely to be taught by well-prepared instructors, as measured by teacher experience, SAT scores, college GPA, and major field of study (Sutcher et al., 2016). U.S. Department of Education (2015) data indicated students in high-poverty districts (both urban and rural) are twice as likely to be taught by teachers with temporary or alternative licenses as students in districts with lower levels of poverty.

These teacher attrition and shortage problems form a continued crisis of serious educational disparities that directly follow racial and socioeconomic lines, having the biggest impact on the most vulnerable students. The importance of good teachers is exceedingly clear, and decades of research findings are unequivocal about the connection between teacher quality and student learning (Darling-Hammond, 2000; Hattie, 2009, 2012; Marzano, 2007, 2017; Sanders & Rivers, 1996).

Lower-quality teaching impacts student achievement, and students who endure lower-quality teachers for two or more consecutive years develop serious gaps from which they often do not recover (Goddard, 2001; Guskey, 2007). Access to great teaching is a critical issue of social justice and is fundamental to ensuring the survival of the educational system and providing learners with needed resources to compete in the future.

Ironically, although funds provided through federal programs (Title I, Title II, and others) and numerous states—including Texas (Texas Education Agency, n.d.), Arkansas (Arkansas Department of Education, 2014), Missouri (Missouri Department of Elementary & Secondary Education, n.d.), and Michigan (Michigan Department of Education, 2017) to name a few—require annual professional development for teachers, the results in terms of student achievement remain largely unchanged (Kena et al., 2014; McFarland et al., 2017).

Professional development alone isn't the answer. Nor is teaching more standards louder and faster. An organizational shift in how schools do business is necessary to raise the level of achievement for struggling students and to ensure social justice by providing equitable opportunities for all students to succeed, and break cycles of lower-quality education that perpetuate poverty and vice versa.

But an important point to make is that improving academic capacity and student engagement is not only an issue relating to poverty or low-performing learners. Joseph S. Renzulli (2008), one of the foremost authorities in the field of gifted education, has pointed out the traditional educational model has produced stagnant academic performance among the most able and gifted learners. Educators often tend to confuse compliance with engagement, and many high-achieving students, as well as their lower-performing peers, report rising levels of disengagement in school. The Quaglia Institute for Student Aspirations (2012, 2014) conducted surveys demonstrating that nearly 50 percent of students are disengaged or bored in school. Rigor, relevance, and differentiation are common refrains of educators. Yet educators do not commonly create environments where gifted and advanced learners are expected and supported to perform at their highest levels (Renzulli, 1978, 2008).

The Study of Mathematically Precocious Youth (SMPY; Lubinski, Benbow, & Kell, 2014) has monitored the progress of thousands of gifted and talented students since 1971 and concluded many students who show an early aptitude for subjects like science and mathematics do not tend to receive the help they need to thrive. Furthermore, the SMPY concluded if schools and teachers can identify the types of intelligence gifted learners possess, teachers can focus their instructional energies to deepen engagement and help develop students' abilities to succeed at the highest levels. The brightest and highest-achieving learners require high levels of teacher support to reach their full potential, but classroom teachers are often forced to devote the majority of their attention to underachieving learners.

Research since the 1990s supports the assertion that setting high expectations and raising the overall achievement and personalized support for all learners are key to providing opportunities and addressing social justice issues between advantaged and less-advantaged students (Audas & Willms, 2001; Burks & Hochbein, 2013; Finn & Rock, 1997; Noguera, 2003). Thus, maintaining the status quo and attempting to simply close or shrink the academic achievement gap are not actually the goals schools should aim for. In the existing model, closing the achievement gap can be accomplished by either increasing the achievement of low-level learners while capping the top, or decreasing the achievement of high-level learners to be more aligned with their peers. Neither of these options is acceptable. A better option would be to ensure proficiency for every learner and exceptional achievement for as many as possible. Raising the academic capacity for all is what matters.

The personalized competency-based model, when implemented correctly, results in raising this capacity by increasing student engagement, authentic learning, and student achievement. Authors Sonia Caus Gleason and Nancy Gerzon (2013) made the case that effective schoolwide implementation and use of personalized learning is essential to the pursuit of greater educational equity. Evolving toward a personalized competency-based model of schooling is, indeed, an issue of social justice because it addresses the needs of each student, removes many of the time constraints common in more traditional models, and allows each student to accelerate through the curriculum as he or she demonstrates proficiency on identified learning goals. This particular system, which epitomizes a public education transformation, has the potential to help schools realize unprecedented levels of success for all students—if it is supported appropriately. This is where the evolutionary triad comes in.

Personalized Competency-Based Education Systems

It can be helpful to think of education paradigms as existing along a continuum. At one extreme is the traditional, teacher-centric, textbook-driven system. All students are expected to learn the same material, in the same way, in the same amount of time. In this system, time is the constant and learning is the variable (Bramante & Colby, 2012). It would not be unusual to hear teachers making statements like, "The term is almost over and I'm trying to cover as much material as I can," in this kind of system.

At the other end of the continuum are PCBE systems. *Personalized competency-based education* may also be referred to as *mastery learning*, *personal mastery*, *performance-based learning*, and *standards-based learning*. Research and practice indicate schools utilizing a personalized competency-based model can adequately prepare students with the knowledge and skills needed to support the contemporary workforce, while encouraging them to cultivate a high level of personal and cultural understanding (DeLorenzo, Battino, Schreiber, & Carrio, 2009; Littky, 2004; Marzano, Norford, Finn, & Finn, 2017). These systems are innovative, student focused, and driven by the needs of the learner. All students are still expected to master the same standards, but not necessarily at the same time. This flexible use of time is a hallmark of PCBE. Students move through the curriculum based on mastery of standards, not an arbitrary pacing calendar. PCBE systems also acknowledge that the instructional strategies that work for one student may not work for another and that tailoring instruction to individual student interests can be a powerful engagement tool. These systems ensure that learning is the constant and time is the variable (Bramante & Colby, 2012). The following sections will outline the foundational concepts, research base, and proven success of PCBE.

Foundational Concepts

You may be wondering how personalized competency-based education differs from personalized learning or competency-based learning. In the simplest terms, personalized learning places the student at the center of the learning in terms of instruction, student interest, and sometimes even curriculum, but does not necessarily require mastery in order to progress. Competency-based education, on the other hand, is also student focused in that students move through the curriculum as they demonstrate mastery, but that does not necessarily mean instruction is differentiated or student interests are taken into account. PCBE takes the best aspects of both of these concepts to create a system that requires a guaranteed and viable curriculum based in priority standards, using proficiency scales and high-quality assessments to measure student mastery in ways that make the most sense for each individual student, while supporting student agency to increase student involvement and investment in the learning process.

"If I get to pick assignments and show you what I know, I do sooooo much better and I like school so much more."

—*Seventh-grade student, New Mexico*

A guaranteed and viable curriculum—what learners will master in the instructional time available—forms the structural core of PCBE systems. It is guaranteed in the sense that every student has the opportunity to learn the core curriculum, and it is viable in that there is enough time available for students to demonstrate mastery (Marzano, 2003; Marzano et al., 2017). This means we cannot teach every idea or skill expressed in the available standards to mastery. We must identify what is most important and essential for students to know and be able to do. To do so, collaborative teams review state and local standards and assessment data and collectively make decisions about what skills and knowledge should be priorities for their students to learn. In PCBE systems, these standards are often referred to as *priority standards*, *learning goals*, *essential standards*, or *essential learning outcomes*.

In traditional schools, all students move through the curriculum at the same pace regardless of whether they have mastered the standards. In PCBE, the opposite is true. Each student moves through the curriculum as he or she demonstrates mastery of the priority standard or learning goals. This means both teachers and students must have a clear picture of what mastery looks like. PCBE uses *proficiency scales* to help students, teachers, and parents understand what knowledge and skills students must demonstrate, while establishing a measurable definition of mastery. Proficiency scales are directly aligned with identified, prioritized standards and display a learning progression that provides students with the road map to the skills and knowledge their teachers have identified as essential so that they can better navigate the road to mastery. They organize standards into manageable learning progressions and allow students to work toward goals sequentially on a continuum and provide a transparent way to communicate a learning goal. The scale consists of four main levels (with half-point scores in between to indicate achievement in between levels), with level 3 reflecting the learning goal. Level 2 of the proficiency scale provides critical vocabulary as well as a progression of learning that will ultimately enable a learner to reach proficiency at level 3. Level 4 provides ideas for enrichment or opportunities for advanced students to engage with the content in a deeper or more profound manner. Collaborative teams in a PCBE system should create these scales together to ensure they are used effectively and consistently with students. Figure 1.1 offers a generic proficiency scale to illustrate the basic structure, and figure 1.2 (page 20) provides a sample proficiency scale for the topic of generating claims, evidence, and reasoning at grade 8. See chapters 3 and 4 (pages 57 and 85) for additional discussions of proficiency scales.

Score 4.0	More complex content
Score 3.5	In addition to score 3.0 performance, partial success at score 4.0 content
Score 3.0	Target learning goal
Score 2.5	No major errors or omissions regarding score 2.0 content, and partial success at score 3.0 content
Score 2.0	Simpler content
Score 1.5	Partial success at score 2.0 content, but major errors or omissions regarding score 3.0 content
Score 1.0	With help, partial success at score 2.0 content and score 3.0 content
Score 0.5	With help, partial success at score 2.0 content, but not at score 3.0 content
Score 0.0	Even with help, no success

Source: Marzano, 2010, p. 48.

Figure 1.1: Complete generic proficiency scale.

4.0	The student will prove the claims in an argument by providing relevant and sufficient evidence and by acknowledging and refuting a counterclaim (for example, develop a claim about the importance of free speech, find evidence that supports the claim and a counterclaim, and construct an argument that validates the claim and refutes the counterclaim).
3.5	In addition to score 3.0 performance, the student has partial success at score 4.0 content.
3.0	The student will: **3.1**–Generate claims and distinguish them from counterclaims (for example, generate a claim about the use of cellphones as educational tools in schools, generate a counterclaim that argues the opposite position, and describe why a person might take either position). **3.2**–Support claims with relevant and sufficient evidence as well as logical reasoning (for example, use evidence from the text to support a claim about the purpose for Walt Whitman's contrasting tones in "O Captain! My Captain!").
2.5	The student has no major errors or omissions regarding score 2.0 content, and partial success at score 3.0 content.
2.0	The student will: **2.1**–Recognize or recall specific vocabulary (for example, *backing*, *claim*, *counterclaim*, *grounds*, and *qualifier*) and perform basic processes such as the following. ◦ Describe the qualities of a claim (for example, it should be specific and should be an opinion that can be proved using evidence) ◦ Describe the roles of grounds, backing, and qualifiers in a claim ◦ Make a general claim more specific by incorporating details ◦ Compare two opposing claims for the same argument **2.2**–Recognize or recall specific vocabulary (for example, *logical*, *reasoning*, *relevant*, and *sufficient*) and perform basic processes such as: ◦ Describe different types of evidence that can support a claim ◦ Annotate notes and texts for evidence that could support a claim ◦ Explain why it is important to have relevant and sufficient evidence ◦ Explain how a piece of evidence supports a claim
1.5	The student has partial success at score 2.0 content, and major errors or omissions regarding score 3.0 content.
1.0	With help, the student has partial success at score 2.0 content and score 3.0 content.
0.5	With help, the student has partial success at score 2.0 content but not at score 3.0 content.
0.0	Even with help, the student has no success.

Source: Marzano, 2017, p. 12.

Figure 1.2: Sample scale for generating claims, evidence, and reasoning at grade 8.

In PCBE, assessments are also aligned with proficiency scales. High-quality assessments are an essential element of any curriculum, but even more so in PCBE systems. In a traditional system, there is more room for educators to assess student mastery incorrectly, as the goal in such a system is accumulating points as opposed to demonstrating mastery. When educators make decisions regarding the instruction, remediation, or advancement of students through the curriculum, it is imperative that assessment be reliable, valid, and aligned to proficiency scales. Thus, rather than averaging scores from tests and assignments to simply determine grades, collecting data from a series of assessments allows teachers to discern patterns that more accurately describe student status in terms of knowledge and skill. Using assessments primarily as a tool to identify student progress on a continuum of learning, and then adjusting instructional practice based on those assessment data, is a hallmark of PCBE and something that leads, ultimately, to greater student engagement.

"What's been great is how we each have our own computers and how we can use them to study subjects in a way that makes sense to us. Some of my classes still teach all kids from the same page in a book—but not all kids are listening or get what's going on. I need to be able to learn stuff in a way that makes sense to me. Teachers need to let me do that and I'll work harder."

—*Twelfth-grade student, California*

Each of these areas (a guaranteed and viable curriculum, priority standards, proficiency scales, and high-quality assessments) are complex and require significant amounts of time to put in place. There are numerous resources (including but not limited to Marzano [2017], Marzano [2018], Marzano et al. [2014], and Marzano et al. [2017]) available to help leaders understand these components, and consulting them is time well spent. In our work, we have seen schools move through this process superficially, which often leads to frustration and the need to go back and begin again. It is important when approaching this process to keep the end goal in mind.

Research Base

The research base that serves as the foundation for personalized competency-based education is rock solid with a long history beginning in the progressive movement of the late 1800s. In the 1870s Francis Wayland Parker began arguing that learning should be personalized for each student as opposed to, as Richard Altenbaugh (1999) has explained, "forcing children to conform to a preordained academic structure"

(p. 275). Educational writer and thinker John Dewey (1899, 1916, 1938) furthered and popularized these ideas in the late 1800s and early 1900s. Dewey saw education as a vehicle for the development of democratic ideals and focused on, as Marzano, Tony Frontier, and David Livingston (2011) have explained, "student-centered education, connecting the classroom to the real world, differentiation based on student learning needs, and [the] integration of content areas" (p. 14). By 1916, Dewey had formalized his theory of objectives-based instruction in his work *Democracy and Education: An Introduction to the Philosophy of Education.*

Education reformers in the 1930s and 1940s continued to develop Dewey's ideas on personalizing education. A major goal of the progressive movement was to encourage each learner to engage with academic content in an individualized way and find creative solutions to questions in ways that strengthened his or her individual capacity for intellectual growth. Even the basic foundational concepts of PCBE noted in the previous section can be seen in Ralph Tyler's 1949 work, *Basic Principles of Curriculum and Instruction*, where he proposed the following four principles of curriculum design:

> 1. *What education purposes [objectives] should the school seek to attain?*
> 2. *What educational experiences can be provided that are likely to attain these purposes [objectives]?*
> 3. *How can these educational experiences be effectively organized?*
> 4. *How can we determine whether these purposes are being attained? (p. 1)*

In short, education was meant to be personalized.

In the 1970s, educational psychologist Benjamin S. Bloom (1971, 1977) presented an in-depth analysis of personal mastery and theorized virtually every student could attain mastery of any learning task if he or she was provided with the appropriate setting and necessary time to succeed. More recent educational research has clearly demonstrated the efficacy of pursuing mastery goals in terms of student achievement. University of Sydney professor Andrew J. Martin (2006, 2012a) argued pursuing personal mastery goals may have a synergistic effect of capturing both student engagement and achievement (Martin, 2006, 2011; Martin & Liem, 2010). Many respected names in educational commentary, including Thomas R. Guskey (2008, 2010); Robert J. Marzano, Jennifer S. Norford, Michelle Finn, and Douglas Finn (2017); and John Hattie (2009, 2012), have spoken to the efficacy of personalized mastery. In fact, Marzano, Phil Warrick, and Julia A. Simms (2014) described personalized competency-based education as the peak level of High Reliability Schools™ (see chapter 5 [page 107] for more on High Reliability Schools).

Despite the long history of mastery-based educational systems, the principal educational binary of the past 150 years has been *time* versus *mastery*. In a traditional education system, *time* is the constant and *learning* is the variable. Students progress en masse through grade levels by earning credits through seat time and reaching minimum performance levels (as low as a D–). Conversely, in a personalized competency-based system, *learning* is the constant and *time* is the variable. Students earn credits by demonstrating proficiency with skills or knowledge on identified standards. *Proficiency* is the minimum level of performance. While there is no single model for a PCBE system, two elements are clearly at the center of all successful systems: "(1) a clear, measurable definition of mastery, along with procedures and tools for tracking that mastery and (2) the flexible use of time" (Priest, Rudenstine, Weisstein, & Gerwin, 2012, p. iv).

Proven Success

School programs based on PCBE shift the focus of schooling from a teacher-centered, time-based instructional protocol to a model designed around meeting the individual needs of every learner. Students proceed through the system based on their own needs and abilities, and acceleration is possible. Instruction initially centers on the acquisition and understanding of basic skills and concepts. Once mastery on those standards is achieved, educators provide authentic learning opportunities in which students apply their current knowledge and skills and work toward mastery of a new set of objectives (Priest et al., 2012). The model is designed to ensure students master required content regardless of the time constraints common in the more traditional school model, and learners cannot simply get by each year with very little academic knowledge and low-level skills (DeLorenzo et al., 2009). The system works because it is truly a student-centered approach that recognizes students' skill levels and facilitates their individual growth toward proficiency of an identified set of skills and content knowledge.

Personalized competency-based systems operate at every level of education throughout the world (Burks & Hochbein, 2013; DeLorenzo et al., 2009; Guskey, 1997, 2010; Littky, 2004; Marzano et al., 2017). A number of U.S. states, including Colorado, Oregon, South Carolina, Maine, Vermont, New Hampshire (Daggett & McNulty, 2010; Khadaroo, 2013), Montana (Schontzler, 2012), Iowa (Wiser, 2013), Alaska (DeLorenzo et al., 2009), New York, and Rhode Island (Littky, 2004), are implementing performance-based paradigms. Furthermore, a number of respected and high-achieving independent schools across the United States have formed the Mastery

Transcript Consortium (http://mastery.org) to discuss how to adapt the model to specific populations. Additional school districts and states are likely to implement personalized competency-based paradigms as results and continued research demonstrate an increase in student engagement and achievement in the model.

PCBE has led to unprecedented, sustained gains in student achievement, allowing the next step beyond a research-based foundation: rising to the level of evidence-based analysis to demonstrate the system's efficacy. For example, the Metropolitan Regional Career and Technical Center in Providence, Rhode Island, is a collection of six performance-based high schools and the flagship Big Picture Learning school (Littky, 2004). Conceptually, Big Picture schools are exemplars of the PCBE model in that the leaders created an educational system to adequately prepare students with the skills needed to support the current workforce, while encouraging them to establish a high level of personal and cultural understanding. The system emphasizes school culture based on competency of skills, student voice, and frequent formative assessments to provide meaningful feedback to students as they progress toward mastery of identified learning goals. The program has met with tremendous success, being ranked first in every area of school achievement, including teacher-student connection, engagement, and academic rigor, as measured by the Rhode Island Department of Education in 2017 (Metropolitan Regional Career and Technical Center, 2017).

Additionally, the Chugach School District, an impoverished, low-performing, rural district in Alaska, implemented a personalized competency-based approach to schooling in the early 1990s. The new model produced skyrocketing results in student achievement, student engagement, and teacher optimism, and the district was recognized for innovation in education with the prestigious Baldrige Award (DeLorenzo et al., 2009). Chugach leaders eventually formed the Re-Inventing Schools Coalition to help other schools and districts across the country implement the model (DeLorenzo et al., 2009). Similarly, in response to the demand for the turnaround of low achievement, the Jefferson County School District in Louisville, Kentucky, implemented Project Proficiency in 2012 with a segment of its at-risk population (Katayama, 2012). Project Proficiency, based on personalized standards-based grading practices, directs teachers to ensure that students demonstrate a solid level of competency on identified learning standards and personalizes the educational experience by implementing individual interventions based on student progress. Results from Kentucky state mathematics tests demonstrated all Project Proficiency schools reported significant gains in student achievement, which could suggest potentially scalable and effective high school reform (Burks & Hochbein, 2013).

Other schools and districts such as the Ron Clark Academy in Atlanta, Georgia, and Mesa County Valley School District 51 in Colorado have boasted impressive gains in learner growth and engagement after adopting PCBE (Mesa County Valley School District 51, 2018; The Ron Clark Academy, 2018). In the Lindsay Unified School District (2017) in Lindsay, California, the performance-based model was adopted in all grades districtwide in 2012. The measured outcomes of student achievement and stakeholder buy-in have been astounding, and as a result of the successful change in practice and corresponding growth in achievement, the district was awarded $10 million in federal grants to continue the implementation and evolution of its system in 2012–2015 (Lindsay Unified School District, 2017).

The Evolutionary Triad

For a school to move forward and successfully evolve toward a PCBE model, the three triad components (leaders, teachers, and students) must be highly developed, nurtured, and collaborative, or the triad will collapse. Leaders and teachers must be equal partners in this work. Teachers are the ones who will make this work come alive for students in the classroom and they will need to rely on leaders who can provide the resources and vision, and help them build their capacity to meet the needs of each student. For example, if a school has exceptional leadership and engaged students, but the teaching staff are not on board with transforming the model, it simply will not happen. Likewise, if students and teachers are seeking real evolution but the leadership is weak or lacking vision, substantive change will fail to take hold. Schools need leaders who are eager to provide commitment, guidance, and resources; teachers who continually evolve their professional practice beyond what they have been exposed to; and students who are capable of assuming ownership of their own learning and education.

The first point on the evolutionary triad critical for substantial organizational growth to manifest in our schools is *transformational instructional leadership*. There is a moral urgency to evolve to PCBE, and schools that do so effectively report higher levels of principal engagement than they witnessed while previously operating as a more traditional system (Ruyle, 2014). For the philosophical and structural shift to occur successfully, it must be led from the top. The only way this shift can happen, however, is through intense focus on improving classroom practice. In too many schools, teaching is a private activity (Schmoker, 2006). In the name of professionalism principals will often give way to the call of "Just leave me alone and let me teach!" (Reeves, n.d.). Teachers need time for collaboration, to both observe and be observed by their peers, and to be comfortable providing and receiving feedback on classroom practice. The more leaders de-privatize teaching in a purposeful way, the more they can improve teaching, learning, and student achievement.

The educational leader must model the change and empower teachers and students to bring it to fruition. This requires leaders' genuine, committed engagement with these other stakeholders. It's easy for leaders to stay busy sitting in meetings, putting out fires, or attending to district responsibilities. Leaders do, indeed, wear many hats, but that of the instructional leader is the most critical one. In our experience, we have seen that some school leaders are intimidated by their staffs, causing them to sometimes avoid confronting various stakeholder groups. Effective 21st century leaders, however, need to stand firm and allow controversy. They also need to express their vulnerability and admit they don't have all the answers but display their commitment to evolving their buildings for the benefit of all learners. Rather than walking down the hall and sticking their heads in rooms, principals need to enter the fray, learn, and help empower teachers and students. Chapter 2 (page 31) presents additional theory and research behind leadership.

The second point on the evolutionary triad critical for substantial organizational growth to manifest in schools is *teacher optimism*. Teachers across the United States have consistently voiced serious concerns as to the state of affairs in education, including the high rate of professional fatigue and burnout (Ingersoll & May, 2016; Ingersoll, Merrill, & May, 2016a, 2016b). However, teachers from a number of PCBE schools report higher levels of teacher optimism than they witnessed under earlier, traditional educational models (Anderson, 2014; Ruyle, 2014). Wayne Hoy, John Tarter, and Anita Woolfolk Hoy (2006a, 2006b) developed the construct of *academic optimism*, which is a measure of teachers' beliefs regarding three facets: (1) academic achievement is critical for all students (academic emphasis); (2) the teaching staff have the ability to help all learners achieve at a high level (collective efficacy); and (3) students, parents, and other stakeholders cooperate with teachers in this endeavor (trust). Simply put, teachers believe they make a difference and are empowered to help their students succeed academically. For the purposes of this book, *academic optimism* (Hoy et al., 2006a, 2006b) will be referred to as *teacher optimism* to maintain a parallel structure and emphasize the teacher role in shifting to a new instructional model, but these two terms share the same definition. Teacher optimism represents a powerful force for school improvement because the construct attempts to identify and cultivate the most powerful traits to best facilitate student learning—which correspondingly enhances the learning and working environment for teachers. This optimism, in turn, impacts the engagement level of the learners in their classrooms, who subsequently tend to achieve at higher levels. Optimistic teachers equal optimistic students and vice versa. Chapter 3 (page 57) presents additional theory and research behind teacher optimism.

The final point on the evolutionary triad critical for substantial organizational growth to manifest in our schools is *student engagement*. Research on the concept of student engagement is powerful and clear: high levels of engagement correlate unequivocally with higher levels of achievement (Christenson, Reschly, & Wylie, 2012; Fredricks et al., 2011; Marzano, 2017). While many schools and districts have consequently undertaken improvement initiatives to increase student engagement (Fredricks et al., 2011; National Research Council & Institute of Medicine, 2004), those that are rooted in traditional education are not terribly engaging for many students. Unfortunately, most teachers (as former students) can certainly relate to the concept of enduring school rather than practicing critical, relevant, and engaging skills, especially with regard to the secondary grades, as academic engagement often declines steadily as students move through the grade levels (Fredricks et al., 2011; Marks, 2000; National Research Council & Institute of Medicine, 2004). A 2012 Gallup poll surveyed almost 500,000 students from 1,700 public schools (Busteed, 2013). The results indicated although a majority of early-grade elementary students are engaged, those numbers drop with each subsequent school year until students entering high school report only about 40 percent engagement (Busteed, 2013). Furthermore, there is a strong, well-known correlation between disengagement and dropping out of school; declining engagement and achievement is frequently more pronounced in schools with lower performance levels and higher poverty (Fredricks et al., 2011; Yazzie-Mintz, 2007). Brandon Busteed (2013), executive director of Gallup Education and Workforce Development, said, "With each year that these students progress in school, not engaging with their dreams and thus becoming less engaged overall, the more our hopes of long-term economic revival are dashed." Chapter 4 (page 85) presents additional theory and research behind student engagement.

Practical Applications of the Evolutionary Triad

Typical research on business leadership focuses on how a leader impacts the *bottom line*—that is, the profits and losses of the company. While this may not translate directly to education, there is a different kind of bottom line that school leaders should be aware of. Research indicates a symbiotic relationship between teacher optimism and student engagement (Anderson, 2014; Ruyle, 2014). Thus, the evolutionary triad illustrates that this connection between student engagement and teacher optimism forms the *bottom line*. When any school implements an innovation, proposes any decision, or evaluates any successes or failures, this is the bottom line to consider. The leader is responsible for maintaining a focus from above on that bottom line and protecting its integrity. In other words, if a leader is implementing something in schools and it doesn't have a positive impact on the teacher optimism–student engagement link, he or she should not be expending time, energy, or resources on it. For example, Marzano et al. (2014) spoke to the importance of consistently gathering and analyzing *quick data* so leaders are constantly aware of the educational organization's health. In this case, principals should be regularly monitoring the optimism of the staff and the engagement of the students to ensure the implementation process is continuing to move forward in a productive, successful manner. As researcher John Hattie (2015) said:

> *The high-impact leader creates a school climate in which everybody learns, learning is shared, and critique isn't just tolerated, but welcomed. . . . There's mutual agreement that any interventions that don't achieve the intended impact will be changed or dropped. (p. 39)*

The findings of several researchers (Hattie, 2012; Martin, 2012a, 2012b; Marzano, Waters, & McNulty, 2005; Quaglia & Cobb, 1996) on transformational leadership, teacher optimism, and student engagement represent a crucial coalition in the movement for substantive educational evolution, especially in the wake of higher expectations for improved student achievement and educator accountability from the public (Anderson, 2014). Schools that have successfully evolved to the personalized competency-based model report clear increases in student engagement as well as teacher optimism. If the personalized competency-based model does indeed lead to improved student engagement and subsequent achievement, there is a moral imperative for schools to evolve the way they operate to better meet the needs of their current and future populations.

Summary

Schools are the most important organizations in the world. Our continued survival and advancement as a species depends on strong educational systems. But, as Robinson (2001) said:

> *The cultural and economic circumstances in which we and our children have to make our way are utterly different from those of the past. We cannot meet the challenges of the 21st century with the educational ideologies of the nineteenth. (p. 283)*

Similarly, global leadership director of New Pedagogies for Deep Learning Michael Fullan (2003) asserted that it is all too easy for people to seek consistency and equilibrium during difficult periods of transition. But rather than avoiding controversy and dissent, he advised school leaders to lean into the danger of conflict and face the challenge in a strong and proactive manner. This involves concerted efforts that engage critical stakeholders to conceive and cultivate a modern system of schooling that will allow all students to gain the knowledge and skills they will need to thrive in the modern world. The effective leadership strategies principals employ during the implementation and the ongoing evolution of an initiative (such as PCBE) increase the likelihood of it becoming the norm in a school's culture.

CHAPTER 2

The Transformational Instructional Leader

Our chief want in life, is, somebody who shall make us do what we can. This is the service of a friend. With him we are easily great.

—Ralph Waldo Emerson

Leadership matters, and its effect on student achievement is substantial (Hattie, 2009; Marzano et al., 2005). However, if schools are to continue to evolve along with the rest of the world, it is important to note the type of leadership employed is critical. Truly, schools are a different type of organization than any other. Schools operate exclusively in the people business and the learning business. Humans are distinct and complex, as are the organizations that strive to educate every learner. Thus, *educational leadership* is, by definition, a complex endeavor that doesn't follow a specific algorithm. One size does not fit all. In this chapter, we'll examine the leader's role in evolving schools, explore the theory and research on educational leadership, consider the aspects of evolutionary leadership in PCBE, and reflect on the implications for leadership practice.

The Leader's Role in Evolving Schools

The philosophical and academic construct of PCBE is not new or different. What is new and different is making it a reality in schools and classrooms. Successfully evolving our schools into the future demands strong leaders with vision, skill, and unwavering conviction. For example, educator and philosopher Paulo Freire (1970) coined the term *banking model of education* to describe traditional schooling, whereby students serve as containers into which teachers deposit knowledge. The PCBE model, however, represents a dramatic departure from this tired, anachronistic system and points to a pedagogy in which teachers in classrooms treat learners as co-creators of their own knowledge. This entails teachers and students operating in a new and evolved system from which they have little or no frame of reference or knowledge of what a different model looks like. Thus, it is critical for leaders to model, coach, and demonstrate an evolved way of operating in classrooms. They must be able to provide the vision, energy, and expertise to bring the paradigm shift to reality.

Evolving schools to the PCBE system requires more than just holding workshops and book studies or hiring consultants (Anderson, 2014). Necessary changes may include schools revising their approaches in areas including scheduling, identifying learning objectives, assessing, and engaging students (Anderson, 2014; DeLorenzo et al., 2009; Littky, 2004; Marzano, 2007; Marzano et al., 2017; National Education Commission on Time and Learning, 2000; Priest et al., 2012). Schools that have successfully implemented a PCBE model undergo a fundamental paradigm shift in the organizational structure that affects leaders, teachers, students, and parents.

This is true evolution in that students must adjust and leaders must empower teachers to learn a different way to do their jobs, and it also demands a new paradigm of leadership to continually sustain and grow the system. Leaders must truly model a different way to do their own jobs and work alongside teachers, as all staff learn how to operate in a different instructional framework.

There is no single blueprint for every leader in every school to follow to lead this critical evolution, but facilitating the tremendous foundational change associated with implementing PCBE requires leaders who possess 21st century skill sets that go beyond managerial and bureaucratic capabilities. Effective school leaders in the contemporary world must clearly communicate a consistent vision, have a high tolerance for ambiguity and opposition, and cultivate the internal capacity to confront the long tradition of educational inertia with energy and fortitude. As Friedman (2016) said:

> *In this age of accelerations, everyone is going to have to raise their game in the classroom and for their whole lifetime. . . . We truly cannot afford to leave any child behind anymore. . . . Leadership matters more than ever . . . a leadership that starts every day asking, "What world am I living in? And how do I engage in the relentless pursuit of the best practices with a level of energy and smarts commensurate with the magnitude of the challenges and the opportunities in this age of accelerations?" (p. 449)*

The effort will be great, but the rewards (in the form of student achievement) will be even greater.

Theory and Research on Educational Leadership

There is a strong base in the research literature regarding leadership behaviors. In their seminal work *School Leadership That Works*, Marzano et al. (2005) spoke to conclusions gleaned from more than forty years of research demonstrating the impact building leaders can have on student achievement. Marzano et al. (2005) identified twenty-one specific leadership responsibilities that each had a statistically significant and positive impact on student achievement, when skillfully tendered. Table 2.1 displays brief definitions of each of the twenty-one responsibilities.

Table 2.1: Twenty-One Leadership Responsibilities

Responsibility	Definition
Affirmation	Recognizes and celebrates accomplishments and acknowledges failures
Change Agent	Is willing to challenge and actively challenges the status quo
Contingent Rewards	Recognizes and rewards individual accomplishments
Communication	Establishes strong lines of communication with and among teachers and students
Culture	Fosters shared beliefs and a sense of community and cooperation
Discipline	Protects teachers from issues that would detract from their teaching time or focus
Flexibility	Adapts leadership behavior to the needs of the current situation and is comfortable with dissent
Focus	Establishes clear goals and keeps those goals in the forefront of the school's attention
Ideals and Beliefs	Communicates and operates from strong ideals and beliefs about schooling
Input	Involves teachers in the design and implementation of important decisions and policies
Intellectual Stimulation	Ensures faculty and staff are aware of the most current theories and practices and makes the discussion of these a regular aspect of the school's culture

continued ⇨

Involvement in Curriculum, Instruction, and Assessment	Is directly involved in the design and implementation of curriculum, instruction, and assessment practices
Knowledge of Curriculum, Instruction, and Assessment	Is knowledgeable about current curriculum, instruction, and assessment practices
Monitoring and Evaluating	Monitors the effectiveness of school practices and their impact on student learning
Optimizer	Inspires and leads new and challenging innovations
Order	Establishes a set of standard operating procedures and routines
Outreach	Is an advocate and spokesperson for the school to all stakeholders
Relationships	Demonstrates an awareness of the personal aspects of teachers and staff
Resources	Provides teachers with materials and professional development necessary for the successful execution of their jobs
Situational Awareness	Is aware of the details and undercurrents in the running of the school and uses this information to address current and potential problems
Visibility	Has quality contact and interactions with teachers and students

Source: Marzano et al., 2005, pp. 42–43.

Marzano et al. (2005) reported that successfully implementing these responsibilities, on average, results in a 10 percentile point gain in overall student achievement. Therefore, acting on these responsibilities and providing teachers with focused staff development, a school community would, over time, expect to see improved student achievement. What principals do has a significant and positive effect on student achievement. Leadership matters.

Marzano et al.'s (2005) findings imply the principal's ability to select the right work and envision the end result is foundational for leading effectively and improving student achievement. Many school leaders work hard but inefficiently because they choose to focus on interventions with little chance of actually improving student engagement and achievement. In this sense, it is vitally important for leaders to remember the evolutionary triad and their role of maintaining focus on the bottom line of the teacher optimism–student engagement connection. In addition to leadership responsibilities presented in the research, we assert that there are professional and personal leadership qualities that leaders in effective PCBE schools have in common, including ethical leadership, mindful leadership, and extreme ownership. These important qualities are presented in greater depth later in this chapter and are crucial for principals to consider and cultivate if they aspire to evolve their systems forward into the future.

Although researchers have identified responsibilities that have a significant impact on student achievement, they also assert that not all of the responsibilities have an equal impact (Marzano et al., 2005; Waters & Cameron, 2007). Hattie (2012) concluded the responsibilities associated with instructional leadership have a greater impact than the responsibilities associated with transformational leadership when the goal is higher levels of learning for all students. Thus, a short review of these two major principles of leadership theory is appropriate at this point, followed by a discussion of a combination of these two principles.

Transformational Leadership

Among others, researchers James M. Burns (1978); Warren Bennis and Burton Nanus (1985); Marzano et al. (2005); Kenneth A. Leithwood and Doris Jantzi (2006); Femke P. Geijsel, Peter J. C. Sleegers, Reinoud D. Stoel, and Meta L. Krüger (2009); and Nienke M. Moolenaar, Alan J. Daly, and Peter J. C. Sleegers (2010) extensively studied transformational leadership theory, probably the most popular theoretical construct in school leadership curricula since the 1970s. According to Hattie (2015), use of the term *transformational leadership* has become so widespread that over 80 percent of principals describe themselves as transformational leaders.

Western Michigan University professor emeritus of communication Peter G. Northouse (2007) defined *transformational leadership* as "a process that changes and transforms people. It is concerned with the emotions, values, ethics, standards, and long-term goals and includes assessing followers' motives, satisfying their needs, and treating them as full human beings" (p. 175). Binghamton University Center for Leadership Studies director Bernard M. Bass (1985) and University of Albany professor of management and psychology Gary Yukl (1989) asserted traditional models of school leadership (bureaucratic, managerial, and so on) are not as useful for school leaders as transformational approaches because the latter allows leaders to effectively transform followers by increasing their awareness of the importance of immediate tasks, as well as helping them focus on organizational goals as opposed to their own self-interests. Ontario Institute for Studies in Education professor and researcher Kenneth A. Leithwood (1992) spoke to the critical role of the principal in creating an environment where such a shift can take place when he said, "School administrators must focus their attention on using facilitative powers to make second-order changes in their schools. Transformational leadership provides such a focus" (p. 9).

The *second-order changes* Leithwood (1992) refers to are the types of changes that cause a system or organization, itself, to be fundamentally altered (as opposed to *first-order changes*, which describes minor changes such as altering a master schedule or implementing a new dress code). Transformational leadership is a critical component in moving an organization along the change continuum from first-order to second-order change. Second-order changes require new knowledge and skills for successful implementation (Waters, Marzano, & McNulty, 2003). Adopting the personalized, competency-based model of education is an example of second-order change in that the fundamental structure of the school organization is deeply impacted and altered. Transformational leadership strategies employed by leaders during the process of implementing an initiative such as the PCBE model increases the likelihood of that new system becoming the norm in the culture of a school.

Some of the qualities of a transformational educational leader include initiating direction, building a clear vision, establishing goals, and setting high performance expectations. Transformational leaders foster higher levels of motivation and commitment to the organization by developing an organizational vision, fostering commitment and trust among employees, and facilitating organizational learning (Bennis & Nanus, 1985). Researchers Kenneth A. Leithwood, Doris Jantzi, and Rosanne Steinbach (1999) stated transformational school leadership can motivate teachers by providing examples of best practice, encouragement, personal attention, and recognition. As a result, teachers begin to feel empowered through shared decision making, which leads to a belief in their abilities to make a difference in the classroom and in the school as a whole.

Instructional Leadership

Historically, the role of school leader was *principal teacher*, with the responsibility of manager secondary to teacher. Instructional leadership theory as an important educational construct emerged in the mid-1980s, largely in response to the publication of *A Nation at Risk* (National Commission on Excellence in Education, 1983) and the subsequent effective school movement. Internationally recognized innovator in leadership development Philip Hallinger and New Thought minister Joseph Murphy (1985) asserted the principal plays the key role in defining a school's mission and managing the instruction and climate in a building. Authors Richard L. Andrews, Margaret R. Basom, and Myron Basom (1991) identified specific behaviors instructional leaders use to enhance student achievement, including providing resources and teaching strategies, communicating a strong culture, and being a visible presence. Hattie (2015) asserted seven major mind frames, or beliefs, of principals epitomize instructional leadership as follows.

1. They focus on the learning first, and how teachers impact it.
2. They believe their main job is to consider how everyone in a school impacts student learning.
3. They believe all learning is a direct response to the actions of the leaders and teachers in a school.
4. They understand assessment is a means not of assigning a grade, but rather providing feedback about the effectiveness of the leaders and teachers.
5. They understand and protect the integrity of the bottom line regarding student and teacher voice.
6. They understand how to set challenging targets for leaders and teachers to maximize student learning.
7. They embrace the concept of learning as a result of recognizing mistakes, and they create environments where taking risks and making mistakes are seen as a critical component of learning.

Simply stated, instructional leaders serve as the school's educational visionaries who must offer expertise and guidance to teachers to ensure all students learn at the highest level possible. In *Improving Schools From Within*, founder of the Harvard Graduate School of Education and the Harvard Principals' Center and International Network of Principals' Center Roland S. Barth (1990) asserted if students are to constantly stretch, grow, and learn, their teachers must constantly stretch, grow, and learn as well. And just as students require exceptional teachers to guide them on their evolution journey, teachers require the same from their building leaders. Although not all principals possess the classroom expertise to be instructional leaders in the traditional sense, they can still facilitate teachers' learning in other ways, such as by implementing the professional learning community (PLC) process schoolwide, offering demonstration classrooms, and providing appropriate time and resources. The bottom line is teachers must see their building leaders as partners in the educational process so everyone learns and grows together.

Transformational Instructional Leadership: The New Paradigm

Instructional leadership strategies and mentoring qualities for helping all staff shift to new learning habits are key for leaders due to the change in the teacher's role from the purveyor of information and assessment in a teacher-centered classroom to a facilitator of learning and growth in a more personalized, student-centered classroom. Thus, in terms of leading the evolution to a PCBE model, the most effective approach is *transformational instructional leadership*. There is solid research behind this specific construct as well. To advocate for integrating transformational and instructional theoretical approaches, Hallinger (2012) stated, "Instructional leadership has recently been reincarnated as a global phenomenon in the form of 'leadership for learning'" (p. 1), and cite research from, among others, Catherine Gewertz (2003) and the Virginia Department of Education (2004) as support. Hallinger (2012) further described how leadership for learning has become a new paradigm for 21st century school leadership due to "global interests in educational reform and school-level accountability" (p. 2). Additionally, Marzano and colleagues' (2005) research indicated the skillful leader is someone who combines elements of instructional leadership with transformational qualities by developing people, providing individualized support and intellectual stimulation, and cultivating a climate where all teachers are held accountable while also experiencing consistent success.

"A really important thing is that our principal just admitted he didn't have all the answers or know exactly what this model would look like in our classes, but he rolled up his sleeves and worked through it with us. He kept us on the path, especially when it got hard. I have huge respect for him because he's a teacher first—and then we all learned together. He didn't just expect us to do it. He understands my job and I trust him as a colleague and a supervisor."

—High school teacher, Montana

Great teachers are essential in schools, but PCBE systems need great principals to lead and develop them. Simply put, school leaders who have the greatest impact on student learning dedicate as much attention to the daily realities of instructional leadership as they do to the loftier concepts of transformational leadership. These types of leaders evolve both hearts and practice as they inspire stakeholders and nurture a culture of learning and collaboration in a new educational paradigm.

Evolutionary Leadership in a Personalized Competency-Based System

Although the critical professional qualities in leading evolutionary change involve both transformational and instructional leadership, there are three specific additional traits we have identified that are more personal in nature, yet we assert are just as important for building and district administrators to cultivate during the evolutionary process. Facilitating and sustaining the shift to the PCBE model requires (1) ethical leadership, (2) mindful leadership, and (3) extreme ownership of the transformation. The following sections describe these three personal leadership traits in further detail.

Ethical Leadership

Modern educational leaders hold a great deal of power and influence simply by virtue of their title or position. Yet this position also carries the tremendous ethical responsibility to lead courageously and make decisions that evolve school cultures and adapt existing structures into more potent models. Transforming school systems demands leaders who are deeply committed to rectifying inadequacies within the existing system. Ronald A. Heifetz, senior lecturer and founding director of the Center for Public Leadership at the John F. Kennedy School of Government at Harvard University, and Marty Linsky (2002), professor at the Harvard University Kennedy School of Government and co-founder (with Heifetz) of Cambridge Leadership Associates, addressed the ethical imperative facing educational leaders when they stated, "Our values are shaped and refined by rubbing against real problems . . . and in the defining moments of our lives, values count for little without the willingness to put them into practice" (p. 22). If this clarity of moral purpose is lacking or not deeply ingrained at a personal level, it will be all too easy to succumb to the inevitable obstacles and revert to traditional practice. Schools are filled with good people who believe in what they are doing, but it can be challenging for these educators to move out of their comfort zones. School leaders will be judged unfairly and questioned repeatedly by a multitude of voices who would rather revert to the status quo during difficult times. These could include teacher unions, parent groups, and community organizations. All these groups want what's best for students, but fear or lack of information can make them resistant to change. It is easy to acquiesce in such moments—a building leader can make a comfortable career out of maintaining the status quo.

But given the deep, foundational systems shift required, leaders in PCBE schools must recognize themselves as agents of evolution and transformation, driven by a fundamental commitment to learners—a moral imperative. Ultimately, the necessary evolutionary change "all begins with the initiative of an individual. . . . A leader initiates, provides the ideas and the structure, and takes the risk of failure . . . while knowing that the path is uncertain, even dangerous" (Greenleaf, 1977, p. 29). While willfully facing uncertainty and "danger" (putting their professional credibility and even their job security on the line), these leaders also demonstrate the ability to lead and inspire others to a corresponding depth of commitment. In 1962, President John F. Kennedy gave a speech at Rice University, in which he made the case for sending a man to the moon. He said the challenge was worthwhile not because it would be easy, but because it would be hard. Similarly, evolving the educational system is an ethical challenge that should energize educators and make them eager to confront issues.

In terms of ways to strengthen our internal capacity as ethical leaders, it is crucial that educators who undertake a leadership role in shifting to the PCBE model continue to constantly deepen their knowledge and commitment through professional reading and collaboration. Another step leaders can take to become more ethical is through networking with colleagues and PCBE leaders from across the world via such mediums as LinkedIn and Twitter. Professional social networking can serve to keep a leader informed regarding the most current research and innovative practices from thought leaders as well as stoke the fires of passion for evolutionary growth. To cultivate greater ethical leadership, leaders can also reach out to leading innovative school districts to learn about errors and successes of peer organizations on the same journey. For example, the following districts may be good places to start making these connections.

- Mesa County Valley School District 51 in Grand Junction, Colorado (www.d51schools.org)
- Lindsay Unified School District in California (www.lindsay.k12.ca.us)
- Highland Academy Charter School in Anchorage, Alaska (www.asdk12.org/domain/3191)
- Regional School Unit 2 in the Kennebec Intra-District Schools in Hallowell, Maine (www.kidsrsu.org)

The weight of leadership in evolving educational culture can become heavy and it can be tempting to revert to traditional practices during the challenging times, skewing our moral compass. Continuing to remain informed, engaged, and connected with evolutionary colleagues is the best way to nurture the ethical leadership that is absolutely necessary to maintain momentum.

Mindful Leadership

Educators and students in schools evolving to the PCBE system need leaders who can bring mindfulness to the change process. Professor emeritus of medicine and creator of the Stress Reduction Clinic and Center for Mindfulness in Medicine, Health Care, and Society at the University of Massachusetts Medical School Jon Kabat-Zinn (2005) defined *mindfulness* as "paying attention in a particular way: on purpose, in the present moment, and nonjudgmentally" (p. 4). *Mindfulness* also entails a certain healthy separation from strong emotions—practitioners are able to stay calm under pressure and avoid reacting out of anger or frustration. This is more critical in the 21st century than ever before.

The *Journal of Applied Social Psychology* reported people's general stress levels have increased significantly since the late 1980s (Cohen & Janicki-Deverts, 2012). Robert Macy, renowned clinical psychologist and president of the International Trauma Center, asserts that these findings are partially due to the increased brain research since the 1990s—medical and educational researchers simply became more aware of the physical impact stressors and trauma can have on the brain and body than they were before the surge in research—but part of the increased stress levels has been due to the massive foundational, social, and economic shifts brought about in the age of accelerations (R. Macy, personal communication, April 2018). A MetLife (2013) survey of one thousand educators indicated job satisfaction for teachers had decreased from 62 percent being very satisfied to 39 percent, and about half of teachers reported feeling "great stress several days a week" (p. 5). By staying mindful, leaders better navigate the stresses of daily life and help students and staff through their own stress and dissatisfaction. The consistency of a leader's emotions leads to trusting relationships and a stable environment. For educational leaders in a healthy organization, all other professional responsibilities center on their ability to remain in the present moment.

Interestingly, a mindful leader's impact on his or her staff is rooted in neuroscience. The human brain contains *mirror neurons*, which cause people to mirror others' actions and emotions (Iacoboni, 2009; Rizzolatti & Sinigaglia, 2008). If you have ever yawned after seeing someone else do so, you have experienced the work of mirror neurons. Brain researcher Marco Iacoboni (2009) further asserted, "By helping us recognize the actions of other people, mirror neurons also help us to recognize and understand the deepest motives behind these actions, the intention of the individual" (p. 56). The educational implications of this concept can be profound. Former teacher and co-founder of the United States' first and largest brain-compatible learning program Eric Jensen (2008) stated that, in classrooms, teachers "who smile, use humor, have a joyful demeanor, and take genuine pleasure in their work generally have high-performing learners" (p. 98). In the same way, when mindful leaders are aware of their own thoughts, actions, emotions, and expressions, they can help create a more positive environment in the larger school setting by behaving in ways that will have a positive effect on others. Thus, leaders can influence positive emotional states in staff and students. If leaders can learn to communicate in ways that inspire and motivate others, it is likely followers will mimic those positive emotions.

It's important for school administrators to recognize that mindfulness is not a panacea for all the ills of society. It is also not a quick fix. But with the onslaught of interruptions, stress, high expectations, and increased anxiety that the disruption of an entire educational structure creates, a quieter mind enables a school leader to purposefully direct attention for the benefit of all. In terms of practical ways to strengthen their internal capacity for mindfulness, leaders can consciously engage in deepening their knowledge and enhancing their personal practice through meditation. Among the legion of books and articles available on the subject, a powerful resource for leaders to consider is *10% Happier*, by television journalist and writer Dan Harris (2014), which presents the concept of meditation from a professional perspective.

Extreme Ownership

By analyzing schools where innovative paradigms such as PCBE have become the norm (as opposed to where they have failed to take hold), it becomes abundantly clear that leadership is the single most important factor in whether the new model flourishes or fades (Anderson, 2014; DeLorenzo et al., 2009; Ruyle, 2014). Leaders must personally own the change and be actively committed to their schools' continued evolution—or it will simply never happen. Good leadership is contagious and critical in establishing a culture of success (Willink & Babin, 2015). The belief that principals can improve schools and succeed at the highest levels is essential, and in this case, allows leaders to focus on the mission and concentrate their efforts on effectively implementing the model. If a leader's attitude toward change conveys the message of "just another hoop to jump through," failure is inevitable. The educational leader must be a true believer in the mission of the PCBE system. People will look to the principal to truly lead the initiative. Principals cannot simply ask people to do new things—they must lead and demonstrate. And if the results are not what principals desire, they must own the responsibility that they didn't lead well enough.

In any organization, it is easy to make excuses and explain why results don't meet expectations. In education, these excuses often include the following.

- "The team I inherited has some low-performing teachers."
- "These students have terrible home lives and no parental support."
- "The district office is always just sending mandates with no support."
- "Our school is already the best in the state, so there's no need to change."

Former Navy SEAL officers and co-founders of Echelon Front (a company that offers solutions in business and leadership strategies) Jocko Willink and Leif Babin (2015) asserted that poor leadership perpetuates this cycle of blame and excuses, and it's easy to revert to previous attitudes and behaviors during challenging periods.

The critical point is that it is not enough for school leaders to simply assume the blame. Great leaders seek honest self-assessment of how they lead and what they can do better. They face the fact that their school's performance simply needs to improve. They don't blame others or make excuses to justify the failure, and they don't wait for others to come in and fix the problems. Rather, they acknowledge the failure (they own the problem) and they develop a plan to succeed (they own the solution). They believe and psychologically invest in the plan and execute it. This is the essence of great leadership and the epitome of what it takes to evolve beyond 150 years of staid historical traditions into the contemporary world for the benefit of all learners.

In terms of what practical actions leaders can take to strengthen their internal capacity and assume extreme ownership, it is crucial to acknowledge the great personal commitment and energy necessary to lead the evolution of traditional schools into a more contemporary design. Extreme ownership entails cultivating the internal choice to move ahead boldly and assume personal responsibility for the success or failure of the mission. Leaders of PCBE programs model extreme ownership every day by asking the right questions and maintaining a laser focus on the ultimate goal. For example, PCBE leaders do not ask, "Why are the kids not more engaged?" Rather, they own the problem and ask, "What will I do to engage all of our kids at a higher level?" Effective PCBE leaders understand and embrace the reality that demonstrating higher levels of engagement begins with the leaders before the teachers, and then with the teachers before the students.

Implications for Leadership Practice

To create the conditions necessary for evolution to the PCBE system, educational leaders will need to develop the aforementioned leadership traits and recognize and respond to staff and student behaviors. Among a variety of traits and behaviors important for leaders to consider and cultivate, the following five strategies are especially salient, and leaders should cultivate them to strengthen the transformational instructional leadership point of the evolutionary triad.

1. Be the face of the evolution.
2. Shape the culture.
3. Bring the energy.
4. Have your finger on the school's pulse.
5. Establish administrative collaborative teams.

The following sections provide details on each strategy.

Be the Face of the Evolution

Of all the characteristics principals of successful PCBE schools possess, the most foundational quality entails their ability to lead from the front and display the extreme ownership necessary to drive the change. Leaders must develop their internal capacity and sense of moral purpose in order to confront the long tradition of educational inertia. Serving as the face of the evolution involves visibility, a consistent vision, and outreach.

Visibility

It's easy for leaders to fill their days with meetings or spend the bulk of their time putting out fires. But teachers and students in successful PCBE schools report the visibility of the principal is one of the most important and powerful changes apparent in the new model (Anderson, 2014; Ruyle, 2014). Teachers must not feel or believe that they are in the process alone or they alone are responsible to answer for failed attempts or unsuccessful practices.

"I love how my principal is so available for us. He challenges us all the time, which can be exhausting, but he seems to show up in my room just when I need it. It's not one of those situations where the principal tells us to do something, then disappears or is busy. This guy is here, available, and takes the heat so we don't always have to."

—High school teacher, California

Visibility, in this sense, is not defined as simply being physically present in classrooms. A visible and engaged leader who serves as the face of the evolution shoulders the burden of outside distractions such as parent questions, data presentations, research collection, and media engagement. Actions such as these embody transformational instructional leadership, and ultimately allow teachers to continue growing and evolving as effective practitioners. These leaders present teachers with different perspectives and new ideas on a daily basis. They also model constant collaboration through regular check-ins and provide a positive, steadfast presence.

A Consistent Vision

The ability to powerfully convey clear ideas is essential for evolutionary change (Leithwood, 1992; Marzano et al., 2005). Principals must possess well-defined beliefs about schools, teaching, and learning and effectively share that vision with all stakeholders (Marzano et al., 2005). Thus, school leaders must not only understand the vision but also live it every day and speak it in every classroom, in every meeting, and to the community at large. The principal must serve as the face of the new model and be ready and able to engage in discussion. In such schools, teachers begin to feel empowered, which leads to a belief in their abilities to make a difference in the classroom and the school as a whole (Leithwood et al., 1999).

As critical as communicating a clear vision is, it is equally important for the leader to understand this is an area that can seem to have an inverse or negative effect when transformational change is occurring (Marzano et al., 2005). In other words, teachers may perceive the principal is not communicating as well as he or she could. In many cases, people equate communication with getting their way, and if that isn't happening during the change process, teachers tend to feel the principal does not hear them or is not communicating with them (Marzano et al., 2005). Thus, principals must be aware that constant communication is fundamental to this model's growth, and also that teachers and other stakeholders who are struggling with the change may often see them as not communicating very well. This can be a crucial turning point in the evolutionary process, and leaders must stay the course. Ethical leadership and extreme ownership demand leaders who communicate what's important and stay on message constantly and consistently. Some practical ways leaders can accomplish this are by sending email memos regularly, constantly engaging colleagues and stakeholders through personal conversations and check-ins, increasing their visibility in and around school, and consciously soliciting feedback from a variety of stakeholders. In these cases, it is really not possible to overcommunicate, as too much is always better than too little when it comes to conveying a powerful and consistent message.

"[The principal] communicated a burning platform for change by continually sharing his vision of what the model could look like. In fact, without his enthusiasm and continued reflection on the vision, we would have likely gone another direction and quit when things became difficult."

—*High school teacher, Montana*

Outreach

Marzano et al. (2005) explained that "*Outreach* refers to the extent to which the leader is an advocate and a spokesperson for the school to all stakeholders" (p. 58). This outreach manifests in the way a leader ensures the school complies with all district and state mandates and serves as an advocate of the school with parents, the central office, and the community at large by communicating the school's vision, transparently sharing data that celebrate successes and acknowledge challenges, and establishing clear goals always at the forefront of the staff's attention.

It is crucial for leaders to be open and transparent during the implementation of any new initiative so all stakeholders understand the difficulties of the change process as well as see the positive results. *Transparency* is a difficult concept for many leaders to embrace, as it can stir feelings of failure or lack of progress. The road to success is filled with difficulties, challenges, and failures—but that's part of the growth process. It is important to honestly ascertain where the school currently stands in the process, admit difficulties, celebrate successes and advancement, and keep moving forward while focusing firmly on the prize at the end of the road. In this sense, it is good for leaders and teachers to have networking opportunities with other educators who are in different stages of the change process. More experienced colleagues can alert others to obstacles and positively reinforce when the team is on the right track. Leaders can access these opportunities by soliciting colleagues to serve as mentors in the process. This has the two-fold benefit of connecting a new leader in the process with a person who can provide pertinent advice and sound professional coaching, and helping a more advanced leader deepen his or her own expertise through deliberate practice and reflective conversation. These partnerships almost always lead to even wider connections with additional experts and stakeholders, strengthening the network for all involved. PCBE leaders can easily connect through such mediums as online collaboration, or more personal connections via conferences, collaborative professional development, and social networking.

Outreach is directly related to *extreme ownership* in that all stakeholders and observers look to the principal for true leadership. It is imperative for the leader to have a deep understanding of the model, the commitment to see it through, and the ability to communicate that understanding and commitment to everyone he or she encounters. Principals and other leaders who have been part of a successful PCBE implementation are often asked to speak to educational peers, leadership colleagues, community stakeholders, parent groups, university faculty and students, members of various boards, and the media about the efficacy of the model, how they were able to accomplish the shift, and what they have seen in reality. In this sense, outreach extends beyond the immediate community to the larger educational community as a whole.

"I have received a lot of positive feedback from some parents. I was worried about that, but our principal engaged with parent and community groups and got good stories about us in the newspaper. Parents really like the idea that their kids will be able to learn from mistakes as they work toward proficiency. A trusting relationship between teachers, students, and parents in accomplishing common learning goals is huge. Our principal does a good job of making that happen and prepping us for obstacles that may be coming—then we are ready for them, and that feels great!"

—Elementary school teacher, Colorado

Shape the Culture

An effective leader builds a culture that positively influences teachers, who, in turn, positively influence students. A *culture* fosters a system of shared beliefs, as well as a sense of community and cooperation. Although a culture is a natural product of people working in close proximity, it can be a positive or negative influence on a school's effectiveness. Some schools have negative cultures that hinder growth and learning. These schools lack a clear sense of purpose, have norms that reinforce the status quo, blame lack of progress on students and families, or have hostile staff relations. These schools are not healthy for staff or students (Fullan, 2001). Conversely, a school's vibrant, living mission can shape student perception and greatly impact students' commitment to their learning and, ultimately, lead to higher levels of student success. Research indicates student achievement can be increased in spite of socioeconomic background or home life if the school's goals are geared toward academic excellence (Hoy et al., 2006a, 2006b). In effect, learner success and achievement can be intimately linked to the school's organizational goals and climate. This commitment requires a collective effort that every member of the school should be aware of and model daily. School leaders can affect a strong and positive culture by promoting a sense of well-being and cohesion among faculty and continually developing an understanding of the school's purpose among staff (Marzano et al., 2005). Specific ways leaders can accomplish this include constantly communicating a consistent vision and encouraging the faculty to take risks and engage fully as they move toward the goal of PCBE.

"Innovation is part of the culture here. The building administration talks about it all the time, and good principals model what they want to see. It leads to lots of positive energy. . . . We were encouraged to try new ideas at every step. Our principal gave us the green light to go forward and explore some of these concepts. If things worked? Great. If they didn't—well, we learned something and moved on from there. And it's amazing how the kids love the new way even more than the teachers. It's totally changed the culture here."

—*Middle school teacher, Wyoming*

An important point to make is that shaping and supporting culture is one of the leadership responsibilities that can have unintended effects when evolutionary change is occurring. People often feel the changes that accompany a new educational model are negatively impacting their established culture and communication protocols (Marzano et al., 2005). Leaders need to be aware of this, be proactive, and embrace the new culture as it develops. One way leaders can address the negative impact on culture during the change process is to focus on affirming behaviors. As Marzano et al. (2005) noted, "Affirmation is the extent to which the leader recognizes and celebrates school accomplishments—and acknowledges failures" (p. 41). The specific behaviors and characteristics associated with a leader's responsibility related to culture are (Marzano et al., 2005):

- *Systematically and fairly recognizing and celebrating the accomplishments of students*
- *Systematically and fairly recognizing and celebrating the accomplishments of teachers*
- *Systematically and fairly recognizing the failures of the school as a whole (p. 44)*

This responsibility requires attention to the ways a school exceeds expectations, experiences success, and recognizes areas of growth. Recognizing failures and identifying areas for improvement is intended not to be negatively directed at individuals personally or to accuse others of failure, but rather to transparently acknowledge areas in which the school is falling short of expectations and embrace that as an opportunity to openly address the need for growth. It serves to recognize the ultimate goal of learning and improving, thereby modeling for our students what we expect from ourselves as teachers and leaders, and highlighting achievement as well as positive movement toward an established goal. As such, ethical leadership is a valuable attribute for supporting leaders in meeting this responsibility, and teachers mention it as being of great importance during the shift to the personal, competency-based model.

"The principal we had when this process started understood the model so well and was so positive that he inspired people to try something different. He was very supportive. He actually worked with staff just like teachers are supposed to work with kids, and he led staff meetings that way. He understood that we all have bad days, could measure where we are, and go from there. We had documentation of our progress posted throughout the building. It felt good for everybody to see growth even during the dog days."

—High school teacher, California

Bring the Energy

Educational leaders in PCBE schools are change agents who authors Richard A. DeLorenzo, Wendy J. Battino, Rick M. Schreiber, and Barbara Carrio (2009) noted are "willing to take a radically different approach to schooling than they have in the past, and who have the courage and moral purpose to see the vision through" (p. 117). Being a *change agent* means practicing ethical leadership as well as taking extreme ownership of the evolutionary process and serving as the catalyst for growth. This quality demands energy, vision, and the utter refusal to buckle under the pressure inherent in changing paradigms. Principals in successful PCBE schools are willing to actively challenge the status quo and constantly model a new paradigm of teaching and learning. Leaders who are willing to take on change initiatives (despite uncertain outcomes) and systematically consider new and better ways of doing things bring energy to the educational program (Marzano et al., 2005).

"We were really instilled with a sense of urgency for implementing this [PCBE model of learning]. Our leadership did a great job of creating that burning platform for change in discussing what was wrong with traditional teaching models and helping us understand what we were trying to accomplish. . . . It made implementation so much better to know that we weren't alone."

—High school teacher, Wyoming

In practical terms, this demands school leaders serve as *optimizers*—people who can "inspire and lead new and challenging innovations" (Marzano et al., 2005, p. 43). This optimizing behavior is the essence of extreme ownership; leaders need to be catalysts for evolution and bring forth the energy for growth. In this sense, principals do not delegate their responsibilities or hide behind the tactic of simply giving teachers time to collaborate and hoping they figure things out. Being a source of energy means the leader is the driving force when implementing a challenging innovation, and he or she motivates, encourages, and inspires others by, as Marzano et al. (2005) explained, "portraying a positive attitude about the ability of staff to accomplish substantial things" (p. 56). Leaders can ensure they bring this energy and act as this driving force by engaging in such actions as celebrating student growth in classrooms and around the school, publicly recognizing examples of teacher innovation and success, recording and sharing testimonials from various stakeholders, and inviting various forms of the media into the school to report on the positive happenings in the building.

"Early on, when most of us didn't see the big picture, the leader's passion for the research and the model was inspirational. It was that passion that got most of us on board and kept us going. I think leaders need to be practical, but they've got to have ideals that they believe in and get that across. Otherwise, things will never change."

—High school teacher, Montana

Have Your Finger on the School's Pulse

Leaders of effective PCBE schools display an awareness of the details and undercurrents in the building and use this information to address existing and potential problems. Marzano et al. (2005) referred to this as *situational awareness* and listed the following practices among those necessary to ensure accurate situational awareness:

- *Accurately predicting what could go wrong from day to day*
- *Being aware of informal groups and relationships among the staff*
- *Being aware of issues in the school that have not surfaced but could create discord (p. 60)*

Situational awareness relates to the concept of mindful leadership and a leader's ability to diagnose and solve issues before they explode into problems. Principals need to cultivate their intuition and skills to proactively address a multitude of situations (as opposed to simply being in a passive or reactive mode). Situational awareness also demands a leader to demonstrate the courage to take on issues as they arise and not sweep them under the rug. This ultimately allows for a more open and healthy school for all teachers and learners.

"It's easy for principals to be busy—they can always find ways to not lead difficult or challenging things in the school. The ones who are always in meetings or in their office sending emails don't have their fingers on the pulse of the school and can't speak to the experience of the kids and teachers."

—K–8 teacher, Vermont

In practical terms, keeping your finger on the pulse of the school refers to *flexibility*, or the extent to which leaders can adapt their leadership behaviors to the needs of the current situation and are comfortable with dissent (Marzano et al., 2005). This behavior speaks to a principal's ability to practice mindful leadership and recognize that every learner is different, every teacher is different, and every day is different. Thus, it is important for leaders to address each situation as it currently exists, with an eye always on the greater goal. Flexibility in this sense does not entail allowing people to revert their practice or attitudes back to the status quo of traditional schooling. Rather, it's about understanding that people learn in different ways and at different paces and having the ability to make adjustments based on that reality.

"I'm in an administrative certification program now. The best thing I learned from watching my principal is how he was able to deal with different people differently, but still keep everyone focused on the same end goal. If people were struggling and upset, he could calm them and reassure them that they were on the right track. He could also bring the energy when people needed an upper."

—*Middle school teacher, Maryland*

Establish Administrative Collaborative Teams

One of the main reasons a multitude of education initiatives fail is because principals and superintendents do not lead them well from start to completion. Research and experience from our own practice as educators reflect that this phenomenon clearly and routinely manifests itself (Anderson, 2014; Ruyle, 2014). If principals and superintendents do not have a clear vision and personal commitment to any particular initiative, they will often be unable to lead the initiative through the inevitably difficult periods of implementation. Mandates for the "latest and greatest" new things are often passed down from state agencies to district offices and into school buildings with very little clear understanding of how to implement them or what the finished products will look like. Often, then, building leaders pass the responsibility for implementation to teachers either individually or through collaborative teams. When principals present new ideas or initiatives every year, the process follows the same pattern, and the school commonly forgets earlier initiatives or deems them failures.

One way for a district to deal with this ineffective practice is to establish administrative collaborative teams in which leaders can engage in rich discussions concerning initiatives, collaborate on best leadership and instructional practices, and support each other during the evolutionary process. Ideally, multiple (or all) schools in a district are transitioning to a PCBE model at the same time and thus the administrative collaborative team is a districtwide initiative that brings together leaders with perspectives from several sites and grade levels. Many districts conduct regular leadership meetings, but the administrative collaborative team should focus on the vision for the identified initiative and the instructional and transformational leadership practices necessary to make the vision a reality. Single schools can engage in this practice as well by applying the administrative collaborative team concept to a group of teacher leaders (along with instructional coaches and building principals) who commit to collaborating, wrestling with issues, and speaking a common language as they move toward an identified goal.

The PLC model guides schools to focus on the following four critical questions (DuFour, DuFour, & Eaker, 2008; DuFour, DuFour, Eaker, Many, & Mattos, 2016; DuFour & Eaker, 1998).

1. What knowledge, skills, and dispositions should every student acquire as a result of the unit, course, or grade level?
2. How will we know when each student has acquired the essential knowledge and skills?
3. How will we respond when some students do not learn?
4. How will we extend the learning for students who are already proficient?

Authors, researchers, and consultants Robert J. Marzano, Tammy Heflebower, Jan K. Hoegh, Phil Warrick, and Gavin Grift (2016) proposed the following additional two questions for leaders.

1. How will we increase our instructional competence?
2. How will we coordinate our efforts as a school or district?

By actively addressing these six questions and their answers, administrative collaborative teams can serve as transformational forces that empower all educators in a school or district as they continue the evolution to PCBE.

It is vital for educational leaders to build a districtwide collective leadership effort so they better understand and embrace the reasons behind the evolution of schools to a new model of education. Consider, for example, the ideas of best-selling author, university professor, and researcher Brené Brown (2012), a powerful voice in the field of teaching and learning and a leading figure in bringing the traits of courage and empathy to educational leadership. Brown (2012) speaks to the tremendous benefits of professional collaboration and the necessity of leaders "soliciting feedback from their peers, asking for advice, and even role-playing difficult situations" (p. 205). She goes on to assert, "If we're not willing to ask for feedback and receive it, we'll never be good at giving it" (Brown, 2012, p. 205). In this way, administrative collaborative teams provide a powerful means to help leaders work through their own feelings, fears, and vulnerabilities so that they could best be more mindful and present with their teachers in order to help them through the evolutionary change process and, ultimately, realize the change we need to see in classrooms.

Another benefit of administrative collaborative teams involves leaders being able to tap into professional support when dealing with some of the inevitable obstacles of growth. In the initial stages of organizational evolution, schools will probably not witness an immediate increase in student achievement. In fact, they may actually experience a phenomenon known as the *implementation dip* that is common during times of organizational evolution. Michael Fullan (2001) defined this concept as "a dip in performance and confidence as one encounters an innovation that requires new skills and new understandings" (p. 40). In order to address this realistic possibility, Fullan (2011) asserted that it's important to "find different ways for implementers to learn from other implementers, especially those in similar circumstances who are further down the line" (p. 75). In addition, Fullan (2001) encouraged school leaders to seek out colleagues who have experienced similar implementation issues, stating:

> *Enthusiasm, self-confidence, optimism, and clarity of vision can all inspire people to keep going. . . . Thus leaders who are sensitive to the implementation dip combine styles: they still have an urgent sense of moral purpose, they still measure success in terms of results, but they do things that are more likely to get the organization going and keep it going. (p. 41)*

Administrative collaborative teams serve as the perfect vehicle to navigate down this road.

"I've had to stretch myself and my own learning. . . . The only way to get through it has been to have a colleague on the same page as me. We would go into each other's offices on Fridays and . . . gather our thoughts, gain some clarity and perspective, and I'd always leave re-energized to begin work again next week. . . . I never could have led this change without it. It saved my career."

—Elementary school principal, California

A final, tremendous benefit is that administrative collaborative teams can serve as effective models that other teams in a district can and should emulate. Importantly, they also give leaders the opportunity to practice the presentation, instructional, collaborative, and leadership skills necessary to lead effectively. If a group of principals regularly collaborates to work through initiatives, it presents a united and transparent front to district staff, allows leaders to engage more effectively with the initiative, and helps them see complex issues from a number of different angles.

One administrative collaborative team practice districts can implement entails principals attending each other's staff meetings and conducting walkthroughs, just as teachers might observe an expert teacher's classroom or medical students observe doctors in clinical rotations. Transferring this practice to individual schools allows teachers to see a united front of all district principals working together and speaking the same language. When leaders can facilitate staff meetings with colleagues, they practice the language of PCBE more often, anticipate obstacles better, and engage in powerful professional growth opportunities.

Summary

It is a tremendous challenge to facilitate the shift to PCBE and bring it to full fruition. Our personal experiences working with schools that have successfully navigated the evolution and realized the successful implementation of the PCBE model lead us to conclude that certain professional and personal leadership qualities are indispensable, and leaders must consciously strive to cultivate them. Instructional leaders who transform schools must demonstrate ethical and mindful leadership behaviors and actively practice extreme ownership over the initiative. In practice, this means leaders must take charge of the evolution through communication and by shaping school culture. They should pay close attention to staff and student responses to change and seek to collaborate with leaders from other schools. In the next chapter, we explore the teacher optimism point of the triad.

CHAPTER 3

The Optimistic Teacher

Nothing great was ever achieved without enthusiasm.

—Ralph Waldo Emerson

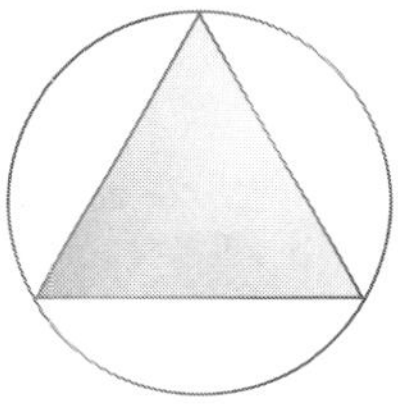

Successfully working through the massive change associated with implementing PCBE takes time and a great deal of effort from a committed group of people. Accordingly, the second point on the evolutionary triad critical for substantial growth and innovation to become reality in schools is *teacher optimism*. In this chapter, we'll examine the teacher's role in evolving schools, explore the theory and research on teacher optimism, consider the aspects of teacher optimism in PCBE, and reflect on the implications for leadership practice.

The Teacher's Role in Evolving Schools

Author and blogger Brigette Hyacinth (2017) asserted that, in the business world, a company's most valuable resource is its employees, and noted the "economic link between employee satisfaction and company financial performance. Employees who genuinely like coming to work every day may have a positive impact on a company's stock performance." In the school setting, this concept can be embodied through teacher optimism. Teacher optimism represents a powerful force for school evolution in that it is closely tied to resilience, positive psychology, and engagement. It has also been shown to be a factor in increased student achievement (Hoy et al., 2006a).

Education is about people, and teaching is about connections. Teachers go into the education field to connect with students, to excite them about learning, and to create vibrant classrooms reflecting their passion. Like Robinson (2013) said at his TED Talk, "Teaching is a creative profession, not a delivery system. Great teachers mentor, stimulate, provoke, and engage." However, teachers often encounter a different reality once they enter actual school systems. Governmental agencies, historically, have often used policy-led, top-down initiatives to address the inadequacies of the educational sector. For example, the No Child Left Behind Act was a federally mandated attempt to address higher accountability standards for schools, with the goal being to increase student success and achievement. The subsequent reform efforts from such initiatives typically aim to change school systems quickly, resulting in shifts of instructional goals and strategies that have broad ramifications on classroom teachers (Fullan & Miles, 1992). But Michigan State University Department of Teacher Education professor emerita Mary M. Kennedy (2005) asserted many educational reformers know very little about the real-life workings of actual classrooms. Thus, those reformers often fail to recognize the tremendous demands placed on teachers, and how the continued additional pressures imposed on teachers are transferred directly onto students, resulting in decreased enthusiasm and engagement. Kennedy (2005) asserted if leaders want students to learn more, they must first address the myriad issues teachers face under the traditional system.

In *The New Art and Science of Teaching*, Marzano (2017) stressed any sound educational framework demands direct instruction to teach new content, ample and diverse opportunities for learners to practice and deepen their knowledge or skills, and expert assistance in applying the new knowledge in creative or genuine settings. These best educational practices should not be limited to students but extended to the teachers who work with them as well. Too often, however, when leaders introduce a new initiative in a school, they tell faculty members it is their responsibility to successfully implement the initiative. Teachers must do this with limited training, feedback, and professional opportunities to collaborate in order to truly grasp and apply the new knowledge, going against everything known about the learning process. It also adds tremendously to the angst teachers feel when leaders impose additional expectations on them without the necessary direction, time, and support to bring the actual change to fruition. Leaders in successful PCBE models recognize and avoid this trap by paying close attention to individual teachers' mindset, practice, and need for support when implementing and leading organizational change. Effective leaders strive to increase staff optimism and focus collective efforts on their school's potential to persevere through adverse conditions such as socioeconomic factors, school funding models, and tradition (Marzano et al., 2005).

Theory and Research on Teacher Optimism

A vast body of research has focused on a variety of factors in schools that demonstrate strong statistical relationships with student achievement. Especially significant is the research of Hoy, Tarter, and Woolfolk Hoy (2006a), who identified three staff characteristics that compose academic optimism: (1) collective efficacy, (2) faculty trust, and (3) academic emphasis. As noted in chapter 1 (page 9), we prefer to refer to this idea as *teacher optimism* for the purposes of this book. The following sections describe these three foundational components of teacher optimism.

Collective Efficacy

Bandura (1977) first identified the concept of *collective efficacy* to describe a group's collective belief in its abilities to achieve a desired outcome. Collective efficacy is the cognitive aspect of academic optimism; it represents the thoughts and beliefs of a school faculty (Hoy et al., 2006a, 2006b). Roger D. Goddard, Megan Tschannen-Moran, and Wayne Hoy (2001) further noted a positive correlation between collective efficacy and student achievement.

Collective efficacy relates to teacher perception that the faculty, as a whole, is capable of executing instructional strategies that will have a positive effect on student learning. Anderson (2014) explained, "An increase in collective efficacy will encourage staff members to work together in order to set higher goals in student achievement" (p. 21). This is a critical area of focus for leaders to ensure a staff grow together in order to constantly improve their educational model. The most powerful yet simple methods to consider for ways leaders can foster collective efficacy among their staff are similar to interventions teachers should use in their classes to build student self-efficacy—for example, purposefully allocating regular and sufficient time for teachers to engage in professional collaboration, providing clear organizational goals, and celebrating success as staff go through the process of building their internal capacity as experts in the art of teaching and learning.

Faculty Trust

Faculty trust influences the inherent trust relationship among teachers, students, and parents. Hoy and his colleagues (2006a, 2006b) described this trait as the emotional aspect of academic optimism in that it involves people making themselves vulnerable to others, with the corresponding hope that the others will act in a manner that displays understanding and connection and is in the original person's best interest. Faculty trust represents attitudes and actions that originate from the teachers, but ultimately include students and parents as well. Faculty trust leads to greater levels of student learning due to the fact that parents and students believe their teachers are good-hearted, highly skilled, reliable, honest, and transparent in their classroom practices, and teachers believe parents and students care about education, strive for success, and give their best effort (Hoy et al., 2006b).

Goddard and his colleagues (2001) first presented positive correlations between faculty trust and student achievement via a series of studies in elementary schools in 2001, and Page A. Smith, Hoy, and Scott R. Sweetland (2001) shared similar findings in a study focusing on high schools. The establishment of a positive, trusting relationship is crucial to the individual learning process in that active collaboration among teachers, students, and parents is important in order to help students set goals and reach increased levels of achievement (Hoy, 2002). Hoy and his colleagues (2006b) also pointed to high levels of faculty trust having a positive impact on student attendance, and Douglas Reeves (2002) suggested that it has a similar impact on increased levels of student motivation and engagement. Increased faculty trust promotes an understanding among teachers, parents, and students that the academic tasks being completed are important and worthwhile.

Leaders can have the most impact with increasing faculty trust by fostering relationships among stakeholders to support the human culture of the organization. This includes implementing personalized educational experiences for students to allow trust to naturally build between students and teachers. In addition, encouraging purposeful parent involvement strategies such as regular, personal communications and ensuring students are able to explain to their parents what is happening in their classes will have a dramatic effect. Leaders who can model these behaviors with their staffs will set the stage for increased levels of faculty trust.

Academic Emphasis

A positive correlation between high but achievable academic goals and subsequent student academic achievement has been established through a solid research base (Goddard, Sweetland, & Hoy, 2000; Martin, 2006; Marzano, 2007). Hoy and his colleagues (2006a, 2006b) have referred to this concept in schools as *academic emphasis* and have identified it as the behavioral component of teacher optimism in that it reflects the perceptions and actions of the school faculty in regard to high expectations in terms of student achievement and excellence. Furthermore, increased levels of academic emphasis can help create a school climate that can "encourage both teachers and students to plan more, persist longer, accept responsibility for achievement, and overcome temporary setbacks" (Goddard, Sweetland, et al., 2000, p. 698).

In other words, when teachers deeply believe in their collective ability to positively impact student academic achievement, and when the students trust their teachers and believe that the work they are completing is important, both sides exist in a symbiotic relationship that facilitates an increase in academic emphasis.

A leader's personal involvement as an exceptional instructional leader, especially in the areas of knowledge and involvement of curriculum, instruction, and assessment practices, will have a profound effect on increasing the overall academic emphasis of a school organization and could, ultimately, help raise the level of teacher optimism.

Teacher Optimism in a Personalized Competency-Based System

To identify optimistic teachers, leaders should look for those who convey the beliefs that academic achievement is critical for all students (academic emphasis), that the teaching staff have the ability to help all learners achieve at a high level (collective efficacy), and that students, parents, and other stakeholders can be trusted to cooperate with them in this endeavor (trust). Simply put, optimistic teachers are those who believe that they make a difference and are empowered to help their students succeed academically.

The shift from a teacher-centered school to a learner-centered environment that the PCBE model advocates can have a dramatic positive effect on teacher optimism. Teachers working in effective PCBE programs clearly state the model's tremendous impact on the engagement level of their students has a corresponding effect on their own levels of teacher optimism (Anderson, 2014; Ruyle, 2014). This reinforces the critically important teacher optimism–student engagement connection, which forms the bottom line of the evolutionary triad. As Bramante and Colby (2012) stated, "The good news for educators is that a 21st century, anytime, anyplace, anyhow, any pace, student-centered, move-on-when-ready model will rekindle the idealism that inspired most educators to enter the profession in the first place" (p. 62).

The idea that increased levels of academic optimism are pervasive among teachers in the PCBE system is important and compelling. The higher level of student engagement teachers witness in the PCBE model tends to increase their own levels of engagement. While no single educational model can cure all the ills of modern society, there is now a way to educate learners that works better for them and for teachers. A constant refrain of teachers in the PCBE model is "I cannot go back to teaching the old way anymore. If I were ever to move, I'd need to find a school that uses personalized competency-based education, or I'd get into a new line of work."

"My teachers here [in this program] are more in-tune with kids than most other teachers. They are more helpful, and they know me better, so I work harder for them."

—*Ninth-grade student, Guam*

Collaborative efforts toward academic emphasis factor largely into PCBE systems, and this collaboration additionally reinforces teacher optimism. The shift to PCBE requires a significant amount of curriculum work, including identifying priority standards, describing what mastery of those standards looks like, and creating ways for students to demonstrate their understanding. While there are many ways to accomplish these foundational pieces, having teams of teachers collaborate on all of them has the potential to shift culture and send a clear message that academics are important in the school. But curriculum work is never truly done. Each year, teacher teams should review both state and local assessment data; make decisions regarding alignment and assessment rigor; and continue to revise and improve proficiency scales. Developing proficiency scales is the most important initial work for schools evolving to PCBE, and it is the critical component with which teachers and students must become fluent. The proficiency scale is foundational in that it is the organic document that will guide all instruction, learning, assessing, and subsequent interventions. It serves, essentially, as an applied learning progression that brings a learning goal or prioritized standard to life. As its importance in the educational process is paramount, it is crucial that teachers have the necessary time and support to understand, customize, revise, and utilize it effectively. See chapter 1 (page 9) for a discussion of the structural design of proficiency scales and to access examples and recommended resources for further reading on developing and implementing these tools. As this work moves forward, it continually sends the message to all stakeholders that the school has a collective academic focus.

Likewise, the shift to a PCBE system influences the faculty trust component of academic optimism. Teachers and parents know children do not learn at the same pace. Under the traditional system, teachers are too often pushed to cover material based on a predetermined pacing guide regardless of whether students actually learn, which is demoralizing not only for teachers but also for students and parents. It's no wonder relationships between schools and parents can become strained as each party struggles to reconcile the goal of ensuring learning for all students with the reality of the outcome. In the PCBE system, there is an inherent agreement among students, teachers, and parents that begins when first identifying learning goals taken from state or national academic standards. All through the process, educators establish which specific student learning goals are non-negotiable in each content area and at each level. But everything truly shifts when the work moves into the classroom with the understanding that all students will reach the agreed-on goal. This commitment to each student builds a level of trust that can be difficult to achieve in a traditional model—trust between teachers and students as well as parents.

"I still get the same level of frustration sometimes, but I definitely feel I can take kids higher here because I know them better and they know exactly what to do and how to get help."

—*Middle school teacher, California*

Finally, the collective efficacy component of teacher optimism becomes apparent in the PCBE system as the shift allows for learning to become the constant. When students learn at a pace that is appropriate for them, they experience success. Yes, they may struggle, get stuck, or even stall from time to time, but the consistent message is if they keep at it, they will succeed. The same is true for teachers. When all students are making progress and achieving their goals, it builds the teachers' understanding that their efforts are having an impact on every student and increases the sense of collective efficacy.

Authentic learning occurs when teachers have identified the critical skills and content students should learn, provided high-quality instruction, administered formative assessments to gauge student progress, and immediately adjusted instructional strategies based on reliable and valid assessment data. This student learning–focused process can have inspiring results, as authors and educators Richard Strong, Harvey F. Silver, and Amy Robinson (1995) noted:

> *By seeking to break down boundaries between teacher and teacher, teacher and student, student and the learning process, we will learn what students want and need. As a result, more and more teachers may go to bed at night remembering the images of wonder, enthusiasm, and perseverance on the faces of their students. (p. 12)*

This is the epitome of teacher optimism that is inherent in the PCBE model and forms the absolute foundation for evolving schools into the future.

"I'm always trying to find ways to engage kids with the content. [Our school] is so much different than it used to be. The sleepers don't exist anymore. I can't say that all students are engaged, but it's getting better and better every year. And that's exciting. It makes me more optimistic about what I do and how successful our kids can be."

—*High school teacher, California*

Implications for Leadership Practice

The demand to meet the needs of every learner and create truly student-centered classrooms is pressing in virtually every school, but the practical guidance of what it looks like or how to make it happen in actual classrooms is conspicuously lacking on a national level. As stated previously, in our experience, the vast majority of teachers do not disagree philosophically with the shift to PCBE. The concept of teaching not as *I taught it* but rather as *they've got it* resonates powerfully with teachers. In fact, most teachers are exceedingly excited to implement the PCBE model, but many simply don't know what it looks like in the classroom and, thus, don't know how to perform their jobs differently than they do under the traditional system. Also, many teachers don't feel the administration supports or effectively leads them, and they can be afraid to make mistakes (Anderson, 2014; Ruyle, 2014). This is why principals need to create collegial learning environments for teachers, focused on everyone pulling together in a common direction, to enhance collective efficacy in the staff, thereby increasing teacher optimism. A leader's job is to coach teachers on the new model and teach them how to operate a learner-centered environment.

A range of factors influence teachers' work environments, but principals can organize their schools and act in ways that improve working conditions and help increase teacher optimism. If leaders can help teachers see how they can get better, they could be motivated to change and, thus, increase their own optimism and engagement. In order to motivate teachers to truly evolve their professional practice, educational leaders must tap into motivational factors and help teachers increase their mastery of the incredibly complex craft of teaching. Working conditions are an important component for keeping people engaged and optimistic in their profession. So, the main focus of leadership practice around this point of the evolutionary triad involves increasing teacher optimism by improving working conditions. There are a number of specific actions principals can do to develop structures and processes to enhance working conditions and empower teachers to do their jobs more effectively. The following six actions are especially salient, and leaders should recognize and address them as powerful strategies to strengthen the teacher optimism point of the evolutionary triad.

1. Understanding teacher resistance to change
2. Providing time
3. Reallocating resources
4. Being personally involved in developing curriculum, instruction, and assessment
5. Fostering a professional, collaborative culture
6. Creating observation opportunities and cultivating demonstration classrooms

We discuss each strategy in detail in the following sections.

Understanding Teacher Resistance to Change

Even with promising results emerging from research on PCBE, the actual change process in schools remains difficult for teachers to navigate (Anderson, 2014; DeLorenzo et al., 2009; Marzano et al., 2017). It can be disheartening for leaders to realize that, although the teachers in their building can eloquently state their frustrations regarding the shortcomings of the traditional school system, those same teachers can also display great reluctance to embrace growth, innovation, and a different paradigm. In fact, many leaders may even face backlash, open resistance, and obstruction against the evolution they are trying to bring about. Change can be difficult, and people respond to it in different ways.

It's important for leaders to understand that these challenging reactions are completely normal. In fact, when teachers feel as though they are at the mercy of forces beyond their control, there is a physiological component to their inevitable resistance (R. Macy, personal communication, April 2018). When people feel fearful, challenged, or threatened, their brains shift into fight-or-flight mode. Once that happens, rational thought and personal reflection shut down. Thus, when placed in stressful or challenging situations, people tend to react emotionally rather than reflect using calm, reasoned thinking (R. Macy, personal communication, April 2018).

Furthermore, the social scientists Carol Tavris and Elliot Aronson (2007) claimed the human brain is psychologically designed to make people believe they are always right—even when directly confronted with overwhelming evidence to the contrary. Even when the brain is able to absorb new ideologies, old habits die hard. In terms of mandated initiatives in schools, teachers are more apt to adjust the reform efforts to fit within the prevailing educational structure than to personally make changes that actually follow the spirit of the reform in order to alter the existing paradigm. Interviews with U.S. teachers produce arguments such as the following (Anderson, 2014; Ruyle, 2014).

- "We don't have the time to do our jobs as it is. How can we be expected to learn and grow and evolve when we are just barely keeping our heads above water?"
- "We've already tried this stuff before. In fact, we have done so much of this work already, but the documents we created sit in some office somewhere downtown, never to be seen again."
- "We can always get better and improve our practice. I subscribe to educational journals and try things all the time, but most of my colleagues don't."
- "The issues are with the parents and the kids. It's an age of enabling and a lack of willingness to work hard that is causing the problems. It's the kids—not us!"
- "Educational research is all theoretical and doesn't apply to the real world that I encounter every day."
- "All these problems I hear about in schools don't relate to me. My kids show up and do their work every day."
- "Administrators are always pushing the flavor of the month in terms of the new buzzword. They're always putting more on our plate and never taking anything off!"

There are some common themes in these arguments that are important to recognize, such as the feelings teachers often express of being overwhelmed and lacking time to get the job done, and not feeling that their efforts as professionals are understood or appreciated. But, more important, when teachers express concerns about administrators always pushing something new that will soon be forgotten, they are talking about trust. Experience has taught them they are unlikely to receive the support they need to be successful in the new model and this too shall pass.

Clearly, for leaders evolving their schools, the personal, human interaction piece involved with educational organizations and cultures is an important component to consider. Fullan (2007, 2008) noted that many teachers may initially resist the level of change needed to successfully implement innovative educational models and foster new cultures. This is especially true for those teachers who have experienced a multitude of new initiatives and reform efforts throughout their careers, only to bear witness to the initiatives' subsequent failure. Furthermore, Gene E. Hall and Shirley M. Hord (2011) asserted that evolving the culture and traditional practices of a school can actually result in a profound sense of loss and grief among teachers, which may easily be mistakenly perceived as resistance to change.

Teachers' attitudes toward a proposed reform are crucial for its success. The vast majority of educators willingly accept that schools are in need of evolution, but some are averse to changing their own personal teaching and classroom practices; some doubt they will receive support and commitment from their administrators; and others simply may not know how to implement the changes in their daily work. Most teachers also have a limited frame of reference—they only know what they've been exposed to, and the traditional, Industrial Age model of schools is what they know. So, to ask teachers to fully participate and effectively change how they do things in their classrooms without regular guidance and feedback is unrealistic. Think of athletes trying to change how they perform a skill—they need constant coaching and feedback, and they still can only commit the new skill to habit when they realize the growth and personally feel they now have mastered a better practice. Change is hard!

Fullan (2008) noted that leaders' transparency rules when addressing teachers' natural resistance to change; it is important to be clear about the purpose for the change and the expectations for teachers' roles and responsibilities. He further emphasized the importance of capacity building among the staff and stakeholders by offering opportunities to build their knowledge and skills and hiring those who have potential to enact the desired change, and ensuring that leaders personally involve themselves in evaluating each teacher or principal's progress (Fullan, 2008). The result of these actions in the PCBE model is teachers who are better able to teach students rather than to simply teach content. Educators we have personally spoken with throughout the United States consistently speak to how liberating and energizing this reality is for them, which is also powerfully illustrated in higher levels of academic optimism.

Providing Time

Time, especially the lack thereof, is a burdensome issue in all sectors of education. Norwegian authors and researchers Einar M. Skaalvik and Sidsel Skaalvik (2010) asserted time pressure and work overload correlate with emotional exhaustion, which is a contributing factor to teacher burnout. In our encounters with teachers, they strongly assert that time is what they need the most—not the newest mathematics book or the most publicized reading program but time to improve, wrestle with what the new model looks like, and watch and learn from colleagues. Time is a precious resource always in short supply in schools, so a leadership practice involving providing additional time for teachers to learn, collaborate, or simply recharge is virtually always successful.

As authors Helen Timperley, Aaron Wilson, Heather Barrar, and Irene Fung (2007) asserted, however, "Simply giving teachers time to talk [is] not enough to promote either their own learning or that of their students" (p. 205). A clear commitment to protecting time must be purposeful to be effective in improving the quality of schools. As stated in chapter 1 (page 9), from the top of the evolutionary triad, a critical responsibility of leadership entails keeping focused on the bottom line of the teacher optimism–student engagement connection. This means anything that does not contribute directly to teacher optimism and student engagement should be discarded. In this case, teachers must be confident in and trust their principals to uphold their end of the bargain by not reneging on their commitment to protect time for teachers to learn, effectively collaborate, and evolve their practice as a team.

The commitment to providing time takes many forms, but leaders can focus on three areas especially powerful for teachers engaged in evolving educational paradigms.

1. Providing time to shift thinking and mourn
2. Providing time to collaborate and learn
3. Managing bureaucracy

First, teachers will need time to shift their thinking and mourn. Many classroom teachers feel they have personally been very successful in the traditional school model, both as students and as educators. They have naturally become comfortable in their jobs and may experience significant levels of angst or even anxiety in terms of evolving their professional practice. Furthermore, Hall and Hord (2011) noted that moving through change can sometimes resemble the grieving process psychiatrist Elisabeth Kübler-Ross (1969) identified, which lays out the five stages of grief: (1) denial, (2) anger, (3) bargaining, (4) depression, and (5) acceptance. In order to create the best conditions for teacher optimism, principals should show compassion and support for grieving staff who may be having trouble letting go of previous paradigms. Leaders can effectively provide for this use of time through regular, personal check-ins with teachers and through teams in which teachers are empowered and have the freedom to discuss the philosophical and practical components of the shift to the PCBE model. Leaders should go beyond having an open-door policy, which places the onus for connection on the teacher, and actively seek out staff members in order to build trust, connection, credibility, and confidence. Leaders must not be afraid of challenging issues or questions, but rather lean into the discomfort in order to help people find their way out of grief and embrace the new reality.

Second, teachers need time to collaborate and learn. Whenever a school leader makes time available for teachers to improve their instructional methods, the leader is increasing opportunities for successful teaching and improved student learning experiences. Just as in classrooms where teachers communicate learning goals and constantly reference clear learning progressions, leaders must communicate goals, expectations, and learning progressions for staff. For example, having more time to learn and collaborate when working to prioritize standards and learn how specifically to use proficiency scales in classrooms increases teachers' feelings of self-efficacy—reinforcing that they can be highly effective in the new model—and those feelings are associated with increased job satisfaction, motivation, and academic optimism. Thus, a principal should take advantage of school structures and processes to place teachers in assignments in which they can have significant opportunities for mastery experiences, rather than overwhelm them with the change process inherent with such a paradigm shift. For example, offering alternative scheduling opportunities for teachers to share common daily prep time can lead to huge breakthroughs due to the fact that, often, when teachers are given the time and freedom to innovate, they explore options and ideas that they never would have considered under more traditional structures. Team teaching, flexible grouping, lesson studies, and peer observation strategies become much more powerful and effective when the teachers, themselves, identify effective approaches based on the needs of their students and the strengths of their colleagues.

A strategy a principal could use to provide time involves organizing regularly scheduled data days (such as once a quarter) and providing a group of teachers or a collaborative team with substitutes and lunch so they have a day to collectively evaluate classroom assessment data and make plans for moving forward. In this case, teachers and leaders are working together to deepen their assessment knowledge, practice their skills in analyzing student assessment data, and plan subsequent instruction based on the data.

Another very effective strategy for providing time for teachers to deepen their learning about the PCBE model entails setting up an observation schedule for teachers. If teachers visit each other's rooms during instructional time and actually engage with students and colleagues in a co-teaching scenario, they will be much more equipped to deepen their learning. Just as with the idea of administrators attending each other's staff meetings so they can more fully immerse themselves in the art and science of leadership, when teachers can collaborate in real time with colleagues and students, they become more immersed in the PCBE model and are more able to speak the same language of instruction.

Excessive bureaucracy, which is defined as responsibilities that diminish productive time and do not directly support teaching and learning, creates significant barriers to teacher optimism (Peterson, 2000). It follows that *managing bureaucracy*, in this sense, refers to protecting teachers from issues and influences that detract from their instructional time or focus. This specific behavior epitomizes the critical position of the leader at the top of the evolutionary triad; leaders must maintain focus on the bottom line of teacher optimism–student engagement and protect teachers from distractions. Leigh McGuigan and Wayne Hoy (2006) asserted that simply by eliminating programs, mandates, and initiatives that do not support the essential, daily work of the teachers, schools instantly remove excessive bureaucracy. When school leaders remove obstacles, stressors, and outside influences, this can increase teacher optimism and, more importantly, allow for teachers and students to focus on the core mission of teaching and learning in the classroom.

The effective leader provides support for teachers by taking full responsibility for the regular functioning of the school—procedures, policies, and managerial tasks. Teachers, parents, and students need to rest assured that evolving the educational paradigm will actually be an improvement over the current system. Leaders need to communicate what the school already does well and will continue, but that the new system will be integrated and make for a much better school with more engaged teachers and students. Marzano et al. (2005) referred to this generally as *discipline* because it conveys the message that this responsibility is perhaps a natural consequence of attending to the primary work of schools—learning and teaching. Specifically, leaders must protect instructional time from interruptions and protect teachers from distractions, which may come from inside or outside the school (Marzano et al., 2005). Mindful leadership skills are critical here as it's important for principals to constantly consider the mantra, *Keep the main thing the main thing*. Also, a principal must consistently model extreme ownership by constantly communicating to all stakeholders that learning and teaching are *what we do in our schools*, and anything that detracts from those goals is secondary. This is also where the power of the bottom line in the evolutionary triad becomes apparent. The student engagement–teacher optimism connection forms the basis for any decision an effective leader in a PCBE model makes; this should be the priority. Thus, this is the time for leaders to return to the business at hand and reframe the thinking of their organization. District, state, or national measures are imposed. Mandates happen. But how schools accomplish the components remains, largely, up to them. For example, if a state test is to be administered during a certain window, then that task will be accomplished and the results will be analyzed. But a strong PCBE leader does not let any of those initiatives detract from the core business of teaching, learning, charting the growth of learners in the building, and responding to their needs. The three personal qualities of ethical leadership, mindful leadership, and extreme ownership form the foundation of leadership practice that truly allows leaders to humanize education, prioritizing the well-being of the students and teachers in a school building first. Collaborative administrative teams as well as teacher teams also become central in helping the leaders focus on the big picture and not allow them to get caught up with bureaucratic issues.

"Moving to this model was hard at first. Most of us didn't really want to invest too much time and energy to it—we've had way too much experience with responding to the new flavor of the month in terms of some theory the district adopted. This is the first time that the principal said 'this is what we are doing, and everything else is secondary' and he meant it. We didn't have to do some of the busywork our colleagues from other schools do—that led to breakthroughs for us and helped move things forward."

—Elementary school teacher, Iowa

Reallocating Resources

Resources are the materials, equipment, and professional development teachers need to successfully execute their duties, and school leaders must ensure that teachers can access them (Marzano et al., 2005). Traditional professional development can be exceedingly expensive, and districts can easily spend thousands of dollars annually on professional development initiatives. In addition, based on our collective experience, we assert that schools have traditionally spent great amounts of money on curricular resources, reporting systems, and testing supplies with very little, if any, evidence of corresponding growth in student engagement or achievement. Leaders' funding decisions should not be made blindly or by habit but carefully align with the school's goals. We assert that there are no silver bullets, and the evidence from our personal experiences collaborating with schools around the world shows that dedicating tremendous amounts of money for the "latest and greatest" curriculum or textbooks has not led to real, substantive improved student achievement.

Leaders need to be ever vigilant to reallocating existing funds as well as seek additional funding source opportunities. Leaders should invest in their people, not simply in the "latest and greatest" thing. This is an area in which having administrative collaborative teams and networking with schools further along in implementing a new paradigm can be invaluable. They can point out mistakes to avoid as well as suggest resources that have worked well for them. For example, teachers and leaders we have spoken with in PCBE schools have often found using funds to schedule teacher work days for data analysis or PLC work more beneficial than bringing in a speaker with little or no follow-up.

This also speaks to using contingent rewards, one of the twenty-one leadership responsibilities Marzano et al. (2005) identified (see table 2.1, page 33, for the complete list of responsibilities). The leader who is cognizant of the power of contingent rewards can be a great benefit to a school. Leaders should use a variety of methods to recognize individual teachers' effort and growth. Such methods could include additional funds or resources for their classroom, administration or parent groups recognizing the teachers in public and distributing donated local business coupons as well as administrator- or parent-provided treats or lunches. Another popular idea entails the leader offering to take a teacher's class for a period, allowing the teacher to either catch up on other pressing needs or get out of the building for a short break. The power of contingent rewards for teachers cannot be overemphasized and they will always be well received when they're authentic and heartfelt. School budgets are shrinking, and even in the best of times, finding money for all the school's needs is an uphill battle, but the leader's efforts in this area can be profound.

"I can't really say that [traveling to a conference every year] made me a better teacher or it made a big difference in my classroom. . . . We actually got much more out of having a couple of days each semester to meet—beyond PLC time—and really consider the data and our practice. The principal made this happen and the cost for substitutes and lunch was much better spent than on travel arrangements or new textbooks."

—High school teacher, Montana

"Rewarding short-term growth is important, because this whole shift will take time and energy to make it happen long term. Teachers and kids need to be celebrated regularly. . . . It creates an infectious energy."

—*Middle school teacher, Colorado*

Being Personally Involved in Developing Curriculum, Instruction, and Assessment

Teachers in effective PCBE schools continually stress the importance of feeling that their leaders are actively involved with them in the trenches when learning how to operate curriculum, instruction, and assessment in the new model. It is critical for principals to roll up their sleeves and get into the deep work of identifying learning goals, creating proficiency scales, aligning assessments with the scales, and adjusting instruction based on assessment data. Being personally involved in the development of curriculum, instruction, and assessment epitomizes the lifelong learner and is exceedingly important; it lends credibility to the principal as a true educational leader. This specific behavior can be a challenging part of a principal's job, yet evolutionary change will simply not happen without highly informed leaders who effectively communicate knowledge of curriculum, instruction, and assessment.

Although knowledge of curriculum, instruction, and assessment is an important responsibility for leaders to cultivate during the evolution to a PCBE model, personal, hands-on involvement in curriculum, instruction, and assessment is even more critical. Marzano et al. (2005) advised leaders to be directly involved in helping teachers design curricular activities and address instructional and assessment issues. These behaviors are the essence of transformational instructional leadership. Leaders don't simply delegate responsibility to evolve schools and classrooms; they are actively involved in learning the new system personally and helping teachers grow and evolve as well. Because virtually all principals were teachers with their own areas of expertise, knowledge, and skill at some point, they may find it daunting to give advice to teachers who are experts in other content areas. But the PCBE system is usually new for everyone, and it is important for principals to get involved in the evolution at the ground level—that is, in the classroom itself. Mindful leaders are humble enough to be in professional meetings and successful classrooms where they learn from their educational colleagues, and then take that knowledge to the entire group. This is the time not to sit on the sidelines but rather to get in the game and have the impact necessary to improve systems.

Administrative collaborative teams play a critical role by providing time for leaders to discuss and become more adept in the theoretical as well as practical issues in education today, making them better able to cultivate, implement, and lead the initiative long term.

"It's painfully obvious when principals don't really know what they're talking about. They talk in circles and it's not clear. You just want to tell them to stop talking! Or else, even worse, they just back off completely and tell teachers to collaborate and figure it out. That's cowardice and nothing gets done. The principal here rolled up her sleeves and got right in there with us—every step of the way. We learned it together and were all on the same page. It made all the difference."

—*High school teacher, Colorado*

Fostering a Professional, Collaborative Culture

This implication for leaders involves striving to create a culture that is supportive, values input, and causes intellectual stimulation. Research indicates positive climate and social supports have an inverse relationship to teacher burnout, meaning teachers who feel more supported also report lower rates of stress (Ingersoll et al., 2016b). It is critical that leaders provide a school environment in which collegiality, collaboration, creativity, and the opportunity to continue to learn with leadership support are the norm. In the following sections, we examine the importance of leaders providing support, valuing input, and ensuring intellectual stimulation among faculty.

Providing Support

Ingersoll and May (2016) found proper implementation of a mentoring protocol as well as regular, personal administrative contact increased the likelihood of new teacher retention. In addition to social support, regular professional collaboration addresses and increases teacher access to instruction and learning resources. Opportunities for personal and professional collaboration and support are critical for the successful implementation of any new initiatives. Principals must take the lead in modeling and protecting opportunities for staff to engage in serious-minded collaboration to identify learning goals, assessment protocols, data analysis, and instructional practices. Tim Waters, Robert J. Marzano, and Brian McNulty (2003) included the concept of providing support as one of the twenty one responsibilities and refer to it as *cultivating relationships*. This directly relates to increasing the level of teacher optimism by facilitating the growth of collective efficacy in a teaching staff.

One could argue effective professional relationships are central to the effective execution of all other responsibilities. Canadian principal and author Victoria E. Barlow (2001) asserted, "Once the leader takes the risk of being open, others are more likely to take a similar risk—and thereby take the first steps necessary to building a culture of trust" (p. 26). Making a sincere commitment to forming good relationships with others is a crucial component in providing a culture of support, and that responsibility begins with the principal. There are a variety of ways principals can cultivate personal relationships. First and foremost, the research is clear: highly regarded principals demonstrate personal integrity and a commitment to follow through on all interactions with teachers and all other stakeholders (Barlow, 2001; Blase & Blase, 2001; Sebring & Bryk, 2000). We have seen some effective PCBE principals carry a fresh tablet of paper with them wherever they go during the day to take notes, maintain to-do lists, write themselves reminders to send positive messages as well as supportive emails for struggling staff, or create and maintain checklists to monitor artifacts from evaluations and observations. Having immediate access to a writing tablet encourages leaders to organize their thoughts, consciously maintain connections, and follow through on teachers' concerns and do what they say they will to ensure teachers see them as someone they can count on. During any downtime, they reorganize the lists to ensure they address all items and do not overlook or forget anything. In addition, trusted principals demonstrate care by taking a personal interest in the well-being of others in the school community and by actively making themselves available to teachers, parents, and students (Blase & Blase, 2001; Sebring & Bryk, 2000). One highly effective principal we know has various times during the day blocked off in which he simply sits in busy common areas, making himself visible and available, and solicits connections with different people in the school every day. He makes a point of not sitting with his friends and associates, but trying to forge bonds with everyone he comes into contact with. If leaders expect teachers to connect with every student in their classrooms every day and personalize the learning environment in a PCBE system, they must be able to model the behavior themselves with teachers, students, and all other stakeholders. Finally, it is important for leaders to acknowledge the challenges of shifting to a PCBE system and support innovation by giving staff room to try new things, make mistakes, and celebrate their growth. Trusted principals "empower teachers and draw out the best in them" (Blase, Blase, Anderson, & Dungan, 1995; Sergiovanni, 1992, as cited in Barlow, 2001, p. 31). Principals can accomplish this by visiting classrooms and collaborative team meetings daily, spending time among teachers and students during the learning process, asking questions, offering advice, and personally connecting as a means of providing support.

These behaviors are the fulfillment of mindful leadership and extreme ownership. The best teachers are not simply purveyors of information but mentors, guides, and inspiration for the learners in their care. The same thing applies to leaders. Schools are in the people business, and principals should cultivate personal relationships and also model the human element they want to see in all classrooms. A principal who cultivates relationships will usually engender trust among staff, students, and other stakeholders and get the entire school to operate at higher levels.

"The principal here is a visionary. He's very hands-on and helps me personally. He's always around, and is a great resource. When we first started down this road, some of the principals in the district didn't really understand it—and it showed in their buildings. If I have a question or concern and I sense my principal wavering in the slightest, then I will not invest my time or myself in it. But the principal here spoke about what we were doing not only to us, but to the kids constantly, the parents, and the newspaper. I know he's got our back and we have his now!"

—*High school teacher, Montana*

Valuing Input

Closely related to a culture of support is a culture that values input. While extreme ownership by leaders is essential, true change will only happen when school leaders are working alongside teachers and students—allowing and encouraging staff to join the efforts at the same level of commitment. A leader's job in this area involves his or her ability not only to hire good people and trust them to do good work but also to seek out their opinions, ideas, and advice. Good leaders know they do not have all the answers, and they value the input that people operating in the trenches every day provide. A school leader should involve teachers in the design and implementation of important decisions and policies (Marzano et al., 2005).

"I can't teach the old way anymore, and I used to hate going to department meetings where people—intelligent people—couldn't get outside their box. Here, the principal listens and we can wrestle with things. He values my opinion, and even if we disagree, we can always figure it out."

—*High school teacher, Vermont*

Valuing input has a direct impact on the collective efficacy of staff and provides an opportunity for a leader to model trust with staff, parents, and students and increase the teacher optimism component of the evolutionary triad. Leaders can gather and consider input by gathering quick data from a variety of stakeholders in order to garner feedback on a pressing issue. Some PCBE leaders we know have established a type of flowchart that describes which decisions educators make at an administrative level and at the classroom teacher level, and which decisions involve teacher and administrator collaboration. When PCBE leaders engage in such collaboration, they don't wait for meetings to hear feedback, but continually and proactively seek input by asking questions, having discussions, and soliciting opinions.

An important point to remember is input can seem to have an inverse relationship when evolutionary change is occurring—teachers may initially feel they are not being heard. Leaders need to be aware of this and let teachers know they are valued colleagues in the school by seeking their input and embracing the new culture as it develops.

"Some people felt that the principal rolled over them and didn't listen to their concerns—but that's because he didn't just buckle under the pressure and stop the change. He listened, he just didn't do what they wanted and that made for some difficult times around here at first. . . . Things are really good now though. The principal always seeks out our input and wants to know how we're feeling about things."

—*Middle school teacher, California*

Ensuring Intellectual Stimulation

Another important element of a professional, collaborative culture is intellectual stimulation. Ensuring intellectual stimulation directly promotes teacher optimism by addressing the collective efficacy of the staff as well as the academic emphasis of the entire school organization. The instructional leader who transforms schools usually has already been learning and researching about contemporary educational trends or the staff would not be in a position of discussing evolutionary change. The vast majority of teachers truly want to find ways to improve their instruction and have greater impact on the learners in their classrooms. Yet, they are still faced with the daily reality of doing their jobs and maintaining excellent educational quality in the midst of change. Thus, the evolved leader takes on the responsibility of keeping the staff informed and inspired in meaningful ways. In other words, the school leader ensures faculty and staff are aware of the most current theories and practices regarding effective schooling and makes discussions of those theories and practices a regular aspect of the school's culture (Marzano et al., 2005). Collaborative leadership and school climate speaker and coach Peter DeWitt (2017) asserted far too many educational leaders who espouse research-based practices don't usually have a solid understanding of the research they promote. He stated the work of such esteemed thought leaders as Carol S. Dweck (2006), Howard Gardner (1993), and John Hattie (2009) is often applied ineffectively due to a lack of understanding of the actual research. DeWitt (2017) recommended school leaders read the research deeply and look beyond surface-level interpretations to learn how behaviors, practices, and influences *should* work. This can be an overwhelming task (based on the huge amount of readily available information), but leaders can stay up to date on contemporary literature through periodicals; books; organizations such as Marzano Resources (www.MarzanoResources.com), KnowledgeWorks (https://knowledgeworks.org), the International Association for K–12 Online Learning (iNACOL; https://inacol.org), and the International Center for Leadership in Education (www.leadered.com); and work from current researchers at major universities.

Establishing and maintaining a professional library is an important way in which leaders can assume ownership over the responsibility of facilitating intellectual stimulation among professional colleagues. If the leader assumes the responsibility of maintaining the professional library rather than delegating it to librarians or media specialists, and can remove more dated or uninspiring materials, this can help to ensure staff resources are current, relevant, and focused on the work at hand. Making digital subscriptions to periodicals such as *Education Week* (www.edweek.org) readily available to staff sets the leader up for increased levels of professional discussion among staff. In this way, a leader can model effective learning strategies teachers and students should display in a classroom as well as model curiosity by reflecting with staff on ideas shared in relevant periodicals and asking, "How could that innovation work here?" As a final example, one leader we know set the culture for his building by challenging his staff at the beginning of the year not just to be familiar with current research but to become true experts in brain research, pedagogy, and the cultivation of students' social and emotional skills. This leader focused all of the staff meetings for the year on professional development and learning, as opposed to simply using them to disseminate information, thereby modeling, again, what he wanted to see happening in the school's classrooms. The impact on teacher optimism throughout this school was profound, as teachers were able to observe greater student engagement and achievement, feel a stronger connection with their colleagues, and see the goals of the school in a much clearer and more powerful way.

"The principal . . . asks me questions [about things] that might work better, or maybe help him understand a situation better, but he's always making me think about things in a different way. Sometimes, it reinforces my thinking about what I'm doing, sometimes it confuses me, and sometimes he makes a light go on in my head. But I'm always thinking now. . . . [The principal] inspires a confidence and calm here, we see it in action every day. He encourages, and actually demands, that I get out of the box. He gives me the confidence to try new things, and even tells me 'you can't get in trouble here for trying something.' I have no fear and I'm not always looking to make sure things are good so I'll have a job next year. He really helps me get better."

—*High school teacher, Montana*

Creating Observation Opportunities and Cultivating Demonstration Classrooms

Professional development and teacher collaboration, although critically important for providing teachers with opportunities to learn and receive support, do not necessarily give teachers the practical experience they need to grow in the model and feel more optimistic in their jobs. It's important for educational leaders to make peer classroom observation an accepted norm in their schools. Doing so can provide opportunities for vicarious experiences, which build trust and authenticity. Peer observation can take the form of instructional rounds, instructional coaching from master teachers and consultants who are PCBE experts, and demonstration classrooms.

Because leaders are often unable to be physically present in every classroom frequently enough to provide teachers with immediate, specific feedback on a regular basis, a powerful way schools and districts can facilitate the evolution of education is by implementing innovative practices in a few highly supported classrooms. This enables leaders to then cultivate and expand the new model or system organically. These *demonstration classrooms* are different from *pilots*, which implies a test of something new in which it's not necessary for leaders to be involved. To create demonstration classrooms, a leader identifies a select group of faculty members to serve as demonstration classroom teachers. Selection of these teachers is critical.

They can be selected from a pool of interested staff, or they can be hand selected by a leader, but it is important that the teachers chosen to serve in demonstration classrooms are capable professionals who are willing to engage with innovation and are comfortable moving their practice into a new realm that may not initially be clear. These are the true pioneers who will learn together as they personally evolve, and eventually model the system for their colleagues who follow behind.

Teachers in these classes agree to faithfully implement components of personalized competency-based education such as learning goals, proficiency scales, and aligned assessments. In return, the school or district leadership focuses extra efforts and resources on the demonstration classrooms to ensure the highest levels of success. One way leaders could offer this additional support and resource distribution is by providing dedicated time for these teachers to regularly collaborate and deepen their knowledge and skills in the PCBE model. Leaders should encourage demonstration classroom teachers to experiment with practices such as flexible grouping strategies, team teaching or co-teaching opportunities, and perhaps even a different schedule within the larger master schedule. They could also provide these teachers with greater access to innovative technology designed to enhance the PCBE model, more intense support in terms of instructional and assessment coaching, and travel opportunities to visit other PCBE schools so that they can personally experience the model in action, albeit in different settings.

Leaders closely monitor the growth and progress of students in demonstration classrooms through academic data-collection protocols, surveys, and interviews seeking their input. Student survey questions should focus on gauging student levels of engagement as well as asking learners what they like about the PCBE model and what they would like to see done differently. Leaders should also monitor other factors such as attendance, discipline referrals, and work completion in order to determine if PCBE is, indeed, more engaging for the students in a class. Likewise, leaders monitor the growth and progress of teachers in demonstration classrooms through classroom observation, discussion, and surveys, and then debrief with other leaders and colleagues. This practice has a tremendous impact on teacher academic optimism, as it reinforces beliefs and validates hard work by providing concrete evidence regarding the collective efficacy of the teams of teachers in demonstration classrooms, along with greater connections with students due to increased student engagement.

It is important to note that all teachers still receive support and guidance as usual during the school year. The additional focus of demonstration classrooms must not have a negative impact on the rest of the staff. Thus, all teachers receive the same support, guidance, feedback, and opportunities for growth that they always have so as to ensure that every student in a school is always receiving the highest level of instruction our teachers are able to provide. Demonstration classroom teachers simply receive additional, focused support so that they will be able to better model the system and help lead their colleagues in the future. Demonstration classrooms can allow leaders to concentrate resources and administrative attention to create exemplars others can observe and learn from. Teachers learn from demonstration classrooms because observing others' successful performances promotes acquisition of their beliefs and actions. Teachers can serve as models for each other, and the most effective models are those who seem competent, powerful, prestigious, and similar to the observer (Pintrich, 2003; Schunk, 2012). Furthermore, demonstration classrooms are a powerful way schools can use vicarious learning and observational learning as sources of optimism. In our experience, just as is the case when the PCBE model is fully implemented throughout a school, teachers in demonstration classrooms utilizing PCBE principles consistently exhibit higher levels of overall teacher optimism than do their peers, and students in demonstration classrooms utilizing PCBE principles consistently show higher levels of overall student engagement than do their peers in more traditional settings.

Teachers also need time and personal support from their leaders to engage in deliberate practice and deepen their skills. Just as in classrooms where students are expected to demonstrate mastery, practicing skills and monitoring progress is important for faculty as well. For example, consider the strategy of communicating clear learning goals and monitoring student progress using proficiency scales (Marzano, 2017; see chapter 4, page 85, for more on this strategy). A number of schools spend a great deal of time perfecting proficiency scales but do not spend as much—or any—time communicating, implementing, and using the scales in real classrooms with real students. Therefore, once the process of moving toward a PCBE system is underway, it is imperative for teachers to begin implementing what they are learning in their classes with students, engaging in deliberate practice, and adjusting their instruction over time. For teachers to use proficiency scales effectively, it is critical they practice using them regularly, receive feedback, adjust accordingly, and practice some more so it becomes a norm. The feedback can come from building leaders, instructional coaches, or teaching colleagues, but the important piece is for teachers to begin using the scales and then continually hone their practice. We've often seen teachers who fear facing classes when they are not yet experts in the PCBE model, but we cannot stress highly enough the importance of learning by doing. Demonstration classrooms are the ideal place in which to implement and practice innovation, as all involved understand that everybody is learning and growing together. This allows for teachers to practice becoming adept with new skills and strategies, and it empowers students in that they know they are part of something innovative and their voice and perspective is valued and actively solicited.

Demonstration classrooms also address recommendations from researchers that educational leaders engage in regular monitoring, frequent feedback, targeted professional development, and intensive support (Weisberg, Sexton, Mulhern, & Keeling, 2009). In an extensive study, authors Daniel Weisberg, Susan Sexton, Jennifer Mulhern, and David Keeling (2009) described the overall failure of evaluation protocols to provide accurate information about differences in individual teachers' instructional performance. We have seen schools and districts assume classroom effectiveness is the same across teachers and treat evaluations as a formality, rating nearly all teachers as good or great, even where there is room for improvement. This results in exceptional teachers going unrecognized and poor performance continuing unaddressed (Weisberg et al., 2009).

Demonstration classrooms can combat these issues by modeling transparency and honesty in feedback and creating experts who will be able to serve as mentors and inspiration as the evolution continues. The term *demonstration* clearly implies that the classroom will be open for observation, feedback, and adjustment. It serves as a laboratory of learning in which educators actively seek and analyze data in order to determine what works and the best course of action moving forward. It is important that leaders build a culture around demonstration classrooms that avoids emphases on evaluation, judgment, and failure, but rather emphasizes and encourages risk, development, and improvement. In this case, teachers see honest feedback not as an indictment, but rather as a necessity for growth and advancement.

There is tremendous need for principals to be heavily involved in the demonstration classrooms and join in the actual experience by rolling up their sleeves and learning new strategies alongside teachers. This exemplifies instructional leadership that transforms systems, as well as extreme ownership, in that leaders do not simply assign teachers to demonstration classrooms with the assumption that they will effectively collaborate and work magic. Rather, leaders serve on the front line of educational evolution. They regularly observe, engage, learn, share, and actively participate in fully implementing a new model of education in real classrooms, and in real collaborative teams, with real people. Leaders can accomplish this in a number of ways, such as co-teaching a class once per week, recording class sessions for teachers and teams to later reflect on, offering feedback and examples they may have witnessed in other classrooms, soliciting input from teachers about what they feel is working best and what additional support they need, and celebrating the growth of the students and the teachers in the room. Demonstration classrooms provide leaders the opportunity to work through common obstacles, learn the process at a deeper level, and become more effective mentors and leaders.

Summary

If leaders expect a non-negotiable goal of schools is to provide improved, personalized learning experiences for students, they must personalize the learning and working experience for teachers as well. When shifting the educational paradigm from the traditional system to a PCBE model, focusing on teachers' intellectual and emotional capacity to carry out the work is of the utmost importance. Teacher optimism is an empowering educational construct that emphasizes resilience and strength rather than weakness and failure (Hoy et al., 2006b) and, as such, has been proven to demonstrate a positive correlation with higher levels of subsequent student achievement (Hoy et al., 2006a). Research shows teacher optimism is higher in PCBE schools than it was when those same schools were operating under the traditional model (Anderson, 2014; Ruyle, 2014). So, in transforming systems, it is important for leaders to keep an eye on and continually cultivate the staff's academic optimism. Providing time, resources, support, and a positive culture in the pursuit of effective implementation is of the utmost importance. At the same time, the evolutionary leader must enlist the assistance of teachers as equal partners in this endeavor—as evidenced in the evolutionary triad. In the next chapter, we explore the final—and equally important—point of the triad: student engagement.

CHAPTER 4

The Engaged Student

If we teach today's students as we taught yesterday's, we rob them of tomorrow.

—John Dewey

The third point on the evolutionary triad critical for substantial growth to become reality in schools is *student engagement*, which holds a position of equal importance in the overall change process to teacher optimism and transformational instructional leadership. Despite intense school efforts and government mandates to reform educational practice, the most compelling perspective in terms of informing the discussion is, almost always, conspicuously absent—that of the learners themselves. In this chapter, we'll examine the student's role in evolving schools, explore the theory and research on student engagement, consider the aspects of student engagement in PCBE, and reflect on the implications for leadership practice.

The Student's Role in Evolving Schools

Educators rarely ask students what they think about their education or what works best for them, nor do they usually give students the opportunity to provide feedback on teaching practices in the classroom. University of Hawaii Department of Educational Foundations professor and chair David P. Ericson and University of Western Ontario associate professor Frederick S. Ellett (2002) noted:

> *In pursuing the goals of educational reform over the past several decades, educational policy makers have focused on teachers, administrators, and school structures as keys to higher educational achievement.*

> *Yet . . . students are as causally central as educators in bringing about higher educational achievement. (p. 1)*

Research and teacher intuition have long indicated engaged students are a sought-after goal of schooling. For example, University of Canterbury professor emeritus and researcher Graham Nuthall (2001) spoke of the intimate relationship among students and teachers when he said:

> *When teachers are asked how they know their teaching is going well, they almost universally respond by looking for signs of student engagement. The look in the eyes, the discussion, the energy. . . . The sounds of interest and focused busyness. (p. 16)*

Unfortunately, as noted previously, the bulk of 21st century students still walk into school buildings designed the same way previous generations operated, with structures, resources, and cultures that often do not meet their particular needs. Nuthall (2001) further explained:

> *The practice of teaching, as we commonly understand and talk about it, is not about learning. The focus of teachers' thinking when they are planning and carrying out their role in the classroom is keeping students busily engaged in activities that produce some tangible product that may or may not reflect, in some direct and observable way, student learning. (pp. 16–17)*

The traditional, industrialized educational system fosters a passive learning environment in which learners often take little ownership of their own learning. Students are grouped into cohorts based on their chronological age. They respond to teacher direction and submit required assignments to earn enough credits to move through school and, eventually, graduate. Accordingly, the core practice of teachers often tends to reflect an antiquated system of beliefs in which the classroom remains teacher centered or curriculum centered. The National Education Commission on Time and Learning (2000) highlighted a flaw inherent in the traditional model when it asserted that all students become "prisoners of time" (p. 27). The Commission (2000) asserted high-achieving students wait for their classmates to catch up, often becoming bored, unmotivated, and frustrated, while lower-achieving students rush through material without learning or improving skills, often falling further and further behind, trapped in a cycle that often leads to dropping out. Even average students are held hostage to time because as their teachers work to meet the needs of their classmates, they have less time for these learners (National Education Commission on Time and Learning, 2000).

According to Strong et al. (1995), all students, to some extent, seek mastery, understanding, self-expression, and positive interpersonal relationships. Far too often, however, as UCLA distinguished professor of education Pedro A. Noguera (2003) asserted, students find discrepancies between their beliefs, values, and effort and the support they receive from their teachers and the broader traditional school culture and structure.

In fact, seeking and responding to student voice can often be viewed as a direct challenge to the traditional power structures in schools. In traditional school settings, teachers or other adults control nearly every aspect of the school day, from the mission of the school to when people can contribute to academic discourse—effectively putting them in a position of power over students. PCBE challenges these traditional power structures when educators seek student voice and use it to inform decisions within a school.

It is clear that maintaining the status quo of traditional schooling will never lead to optimal student engagement, learning, and achievement. Thus, it's vital for leaders and other adult stakeholders involved with the educational evolution to recognize the unique perspective, knowledge, and experience of students and engage them as equitable partners in every facet of the education system. Engaging students academically is a critical element schools must specifically address and cultivate, rather than simply relying on grades or test scores to gauge growth, proficiency, and achievement. The shift from the traditional system to PCBE is a focal shift from teaching to learning. The leadership plays a critical role in promoting this shift. Not only must leaders seek students' voice in order to engage them in their own learning, but leaders must also support teachers in understanding that the shift to focusing on learning rather than teaching does not devalue the teacher's place in the educational process but that their impact will be greater when they support the learning of individual students through PCBE.

Theory and Research on Student Engagement

The concept of student engagement as a focused area of study has increased since the late 1990s largely due to the strong correlation between engaged students and academic success (Alexander, Entwisle, & Horsey, 1997; Appleton, Christenson, & Furlong, 2008; Finn & Rock, 1997). It is clear the more time students spend engaged during instruction, the more they learn (Gettinger & Ball, 2007). In the following sections, we'll examine the theory and research that contribute to how educators define student engagement, point to the need for greater student engagement, and identify the factors that influence student engagement.

Defining Student Engagement

Though a single, universally accepted definition does not exist in the research literature, *student engagement* can be described as a complex psychological construct composed of multiple dimensions, including behavioral, emotional, and cognitive components as well as feelings of belonging, enjoyment, and attachment (Fredricks et al., 2011). The behaviors that spring forth from the energy and drive of motivation can further define *engagement*, and it plays a large part in students' interests, enjoyment of academics, and ultimate level of academic achievement (Martin, 2011, 2012a; Martin & Liem, 2010; Pintrich, 2003; Schenck, 2011; Schunk, 2012). Yazzie-Mintz (2010) further noted engagement can also be understood as a series of relationships "between the student and school community, the student and school adults, the student and peers, the student and instruction, and the student and curriculum" (p. 1). Author, researcher, speaker, and school improvement advocate Phillip C. Schlechty (2002) identified the following five levels of student engagement.

1. **Authentic engagement:** Students are immersed in work that has clear meaning and immediate value to them (for example, reading a book on a topic of personal interest).
2. **Ritual compliance:** The work has little or no immediate meaning to students, but there are extrinsic outcomes of value that keep them engaged (for example, earning grades necessary for college acceptance).
3. **Passive compliance:** Students see little or no meaning in the assigned work but expend effort merely to avoid negative consequences (for example, not having to stay in during recess to complete work).
4. **Retreatism:** Students are disengaged from assigned work and make no attempt to comply but are not disruptive to the learning of others (for example, staring out the window during independent work time).
5. **Rebellion:** Students refuse to do the assigned task, act disruptively, and attempt to substitute alternative activities (for example, talking to others or getting out of their seats during instruction).

In essence, *engagement* describes meaningful student involvement throughout the learning environment, including students' ownership of their own learning and the corresponding impact on school climate. Student engagement occurs when students make a conscious commitment to learning. They try hard to learn what school offers and take pride not simply in earning formal grades but in understanding the material and incorporating or internalizing it into their lives.

Understanding the Need for Greater Student Engagement

Businesses and services in all sectors keep customers and clients engaged through personalization. Rapid advancement in technology and data mining have created a world that allows us to have our individual needs and wants met. In all aspects of our lives, we have come to expect personalization. Learners are coming to expect the same from education, and when they do not receive it, their engagement declines.

International researchers from a range of disciplines, including educational psychology, developmental psychology, public health, and teacher education, have been trying to get a stronger conceptual grip on student engagement (Christenson et al., 2012). Students around the world increasingly report being bored and disengaged in school (Audas & Willms, 2001; De Broucker, 2005; Rubinson, 2004). In the United States, a 2012 Gallup poll surveyed over 459,000 students and measured their hope, engagement, and well-being. The survey specifically defined engagement as "involvement in and enthusiasm for school" (Busteed, 2013). The data showed that student engagement declined from grades 5 through 12, that roughly 43 percent of students are not engaged or are actively disengaged at school, and that more than 1.2 million students drop out of high school annually.

Additionally, educators Subini A. Annamma, Amy L. Boelé, Brooke A. Moore, and Janette Klingner (2013) suggested, as school populations become increasingly more diverse but the teacher population remains relatively homogeneous in terms of ethnicity and gender, teacher-student disconnects will undoubtedly continue to perpetuate student disengagement and underachievement.

There is compelling research evidence suggesting more engaged students may help facilitate school improvement efforts in general, and PCBE implementation in particular, by actively engaging in discussion with the teachers and leaders regarding what works best for them in the classroom (Cook-Sather, 2002c; Education Alliance, 2004; Ferguson, 2002). In fact, many leaders in effective PCBE programs assert that higher student engagement in the classroom translates to increased student engagement in the larger school community; once they take control of their own learning, they are able to help schools evolve to the point in which they are more responsive to student needs and voice (Cook-Sather, 2002c; Education Alliance, 2004; Raymond, 2001).

For this reason, many educators and other stakeholders are seeking better data on engagement and disengagement for needs assessment, diagnosis, and prevention (Fredricks et al., 2011). In simple terms, failure to strengthen students' understanding and commitment to help evolve schools will result in the corresponding failure of virtually every initiative. As Ericson and Ellett (2002) pointed out, "It is the students—their goals, motivations, and conceptions of the good life—that may well prove to be the undoing of the educational reform movement" (p. 2).

A vast amount of research has contributed to educators' knowledge of student engagement. Without a high level of engagement, students are not as focused on learning, but rather often simply follow assigned tasks to be compliant, get higher grades, or earn credit (Quaglia & Cobb, 1996; Rumberger & Lim, 2008; Skinner, Furrer, Marchand, & Kindermann, 2008; Smyth, 2006). Importantly, "schools that focus on student engagement are seeing both great possibility and real success" (Yazzie-Mintz, 2010, p. 2). In fact, Strong et al. (1995) found work engaging for students:

> *[Work] stimulated their curiosity, permitted them to express their creativity, and fostered positive relationships with others. It was also work at which they were good. As for activities they hated, both teachers and students cited work that was repetitive, that required little or no thought, and that was forced on them by others. (p. 8)*

What's most compelling is engagement is changeable and can be learned. Martin's (2006) research clearly indicated the profound impact of educational interventions aimed at enhancing students' personal bests in terms of their engagement and achievement over the course of their academic development. Instruction focused on academic personal bests has the potential to facilitate and increase students' self-efficacy in learning because doing better over time is seen as accessible by students, and this perceived accessibility to success enhances students' efficacy regarding their learning.

Identifying Factors That Influence Student Engagement

These obstacles are not insurmountable. To conquer them, educational systems can support and cultivate a variety of factors that influence student motivation and engagement, including student voice, school climate, students' sense of belonging, and students' intrinsic motivation.

Schools can have a dramatic impact on overall student engagement if adults invoke a radically different ethos that encourages and promotes student voice (Smyth, 2006).

Encouraging results from a Gallup poll (Busteed, 2013) demonstrated the compelling conclusion that *hope* is a stronger predictor of overall academic success than more conventional indicators such as test scores and GPA. In relation to this specific measure, the poll reflected that 72 percent of hopeful students are engaged while only 65 percent of thriving students are engaged, and 84 percent of students who believe their school is committed to building on their personal strengths reported being engaged (Busteed, 2013). As Yazzie-Mintz (2010) said:

> *Understanding students' reasons for being in school may help schools create more engaging learning environments for students, providing students with compelling reasons to persist and achieve. At the same time, understanding students' reasons for checking out of school—either temporarily in the case of boredom or permanently in the case of dropping out—can provide schools with a set of guideposts for engaging students in learning. (p. 5)*

Research also indicates school climate and a sense of belonging have a direct impact on student engagement, effort, and performance (Burks & Hochbein, 2013; De Wit, Karioja, & Rye, 2010; Rumberger & Lim, 2008). This may be particularly important at the high school level, as findings also have demonstrated student perception of peer, teacher, and emotional support typically decreases at the secondary level (Barber & Olsen, 2004; Burks & Hochbein, 2013; Furrer & Skinner, 2003; Marks, 2000; Reschly, Huebner, Appleton, & Antaramian, 2008). So, schools need to improve high school students' self-confidence and cultivate caring learning environments. However, without simultaneous improvements in teaching, improved student confidence and perceptions are unlikely to generate authentic student growth and achievement (Bryk, Sebring, Allensworth, Luppescu, & Easton, 2010). In our experience, leaders can best accomplish this improvement in the instructional capacity of teachers by offering focused, non-negotiable professional development, presented first via training sessions with seasoned professionals, and subsequently reinforced through deliberate practice in which teachers receive feedback from colleagues as well as instructional coaches.

There also seems to be a solid relationship between engagement and intrinsic motivation (Ryan & Deci, 2000), which is generally considered more durable and self-enhancing than extrinsic factors (Kohn, 1993). This concept aligns with what psychologist and distinguished professor of psychology and management at Claremont Graduate University Mihaly Csikszentmihalyi (1990) described as *flow* in learning. Educator John Spencer (2017) explained, "Flow happens in the moments when someone is fully engaged, present, focused, and alert—he or she gets in the zone" (p. 2). Spencer (2017) recommended promoting students' intrinsic motivation by designing projects that connect to their interests and that include creativity and problem solving, explaining, "Creativity not only requires a deeper level of buy-in and engagement than compliance does but also a deeper level of thought" (p. 15). Because intrinsic motivation is related to students ultimately achieving a level of growth that significantly exceeds their present capacity (Martin, 2006), leaders should work with teachers to incorporate such measures in classrooms and throughout the school as a whole.

Student Engagement in a Personalized Competency-Based System

Traditional structures and policies often imbue schools with a culture that makes truly personalized approaches to learning and instruction difficult to implement. The impact of this phenomenon can be profound. Educators Lannie Kanevsky and Tracey Keighley (2003) described a powerful study that revealed a number of high school students identified as gifted in elementary school who were classified as underachieving in later grades. They asserted *schooling* is associated with boredom, while *learning* is associated with engagement. Although educators are intuitively aware of this reality, Pink (2009) addressed the staidness of tradition-bound organizations by stating:

> *As the world economy demands more nonroutine, creative, conceptual abilities—too many schools are moving in the wrong direction. They're redoubling their efforts on routines, right answers, and standardization. . . . We're bribing students into compliance instead of challenging them into engagement. (p. 185)*

One of the most exciting benefits that correspond to the adoption of PCBE paradigms is that these models tend to facilitate an increase in individual student engagement and motivation, as measured by academic and behavioral data as well as interview protocols (DeLorenzo et al., 2009; Priest et al., 2012; Ruyle, 2014). Furthermore, researchers Chen-Lin C. Kulik, James A. Kulik, and Robert L. Bangert-Drowns (1990) conducted a meta-analysis of 108 studies of mastery learning and uncovered positive effects for high-achieving students, and even greater positive effects for low-achieving students. Although it is true that high academic achievement does not necessarily correlate with high levels of engagement in that some students may garner good grades purely as a result of sheer compliance to teacher rules, PCBE systems are designed to help all learners engage at their capability levels. In other words, the personalized component allows for teachers to meet and challenge all students at their appropriate level of skill. In fact, Guskey (1997, 2008, 2010) expanded this research and asserted, "When compared to students from traditionally taught classes, students in mastery learning classes have been shown to learn better, reach higher levels of achievement, and develop greater confidence in their ability to learn and in themselves as learners" (as cited in Guskey, 2008, p. 194).

Indeed, based on our collective experience and personal research, we assert that the vast majority of students in PCBE schools indicate they are clearly more engaged in their academic progress than they were in the traditional system. They learn and internalize content more deeply and are effusive in their praise for the personalized model of instruction, assessment, and reporting (Ruyle, 2014). This is accomplished in PCBE paradigms that encourage students to play an active role in their learning process. They are no longer completing assignments simply for the sake of plowing through the curriculum. Rather, students are using their individual knowledge and personal experience to better comprehend new content and master crucial skills and knowledge.

Through our personal research and conversations we have had with students in PCBE K–12 models, we can identify four common themes that learners themselves deemed especially pertinent to their increased level of academic engagement.

1. Personal connection and mentoring
2. Higher expectations and increased pride in their school
3. A different view of grades and assessment
4. Teacher proficiency with the PCBE model

Students speak directly to these items as being some of the most beneficial aspects of their experiences in PCBE schools. Further, we see many areas of overlap between these student-identified themes and elements Pink (2009) and Kanevsky and Keighley (2003) have noted as being key in inspiring engagement and motivation. Pink (2009) concluded three elements are the hallmarks of true motivation—(1) autonomy, (2) mastery, and (3) purpose—and Kanevsky and Keighley (2003) identified five elements likely to create a culture of *learning* as opposed to a culture of *schooling*—(1) control, (2) choice, (3) challenge, (4) complexity, and (5) caring. Leaders would do well to consciously create an environment that recognizes and cultivates these themes. Thus, the following sections discuss the research regarding the four aforementioned themes, and speak to how the factors of engagement and motivation are embedded in each, thereby presenting a powerful case for the shift to a personalized competency-based model of education.

Personal Connection and Mentoring

First, students consistently rate the individual attention they receive in the PCBE model the most important factor in their engagement and ultimate success (Ruyle, 2014). Although expectations for student performance are higher in PCBE, the personalized guidance students need to reach more advanced levels of skill and knowledge is always available. In interviews and surveys we have conducted as research for this book, students consistently referred to the herd mentality that is common in traditional schools and entails the practice of students all sitting in a classroom following teacher direction. Students often condemn this routine as antithetical to the stated mission of most schools to foster personal growth and advancement. Students strongly expressed that their level of engagement often revolves around the fact that instructors in the PCBE model teach differently and respect their individual styles of learning more effectively than they had experienced in their traditional classes.

Strong, Silver, and Robinson (1995) asserted that "Students who are engaged in their work are energized by four goals—success, curiosity, originality, and satisfying relationships" (p. 8). Students want and need work that empowers them to practice and demonstrate skills independently and at a high level, which helps improve their sense of themselves as competent and successful human beings. This is the drive toward the autonomy, mastery, and purpose that Pink (2009) asserted are the hallmarks of motivation. As students note their progress, they are apt to believe they are capable of further learning.

"I think teachers in the regular classes like traditional school better because it's easier for them to have kids just follow [directions] and do what they say, but that doesn't push kids to be better. They don't have to connect with kids and work with them individually as much. They just have to teach something once and then give homework. But here, they teach in a way that fits me better. This is awesome!"

—Eleventh-grade student, Montana

In PCBE, teachers' work with individuals or small groups can be more efficient since learning targets are better defined, which leads students to understand tasks and enhances their ability to receive the targeted instruction and assistance they need. These students exhibit a higher level of trust in their teachers as well as themselves than they did under the traditional system, and they have great belief in their efforts to move their schooling forward.

Higher Expectations and Increased Pride

Second, students and teachers from PCBE schools consistently report higher expectations and believe all learners can achieve at high levels, leading to increased pride in themselves and their schools (Anderson, 2014; Ruyle, 2014). How much a teacher expects from his or her students has a great impact on learner engagement and subsequent success. Joe Burks and Craig Hochbein (2013) suggested a connection between engagement and students' confidence in their ability to be successful, stating, "Interventions specifically designed to improve academic skills might require improvement of academic self-concept, or the belief in one's academic ability" (p. 17). Herbert W. Marsh and Rhonda G. Craven's (2006) research indicated that student confidence, or self-concept, in terms of their academic abilities often results in stronger student outcomes, and this higher level of achievement can cyclically lead to further increases in academic self-concept, a phenomenon that has been referred to as the *reciprocal effects model* (Marsh & O'Mara, 2008). In addition, according to a 2014 Center for American Progress report (Boser, Wilhelm, & Hanna, 2014), U.S. students of color and students from low socioeconomic backgrounds often have lower teacher expectations. High school teachers in this study believed high-poverty, black, and Hispanic students were (respectively) 53, 47, and 42 percent less likely to graduate from college compared to their more affluent or white peers (Boser et al., 2014). Furthermore, National Center for Education Statistics researchers asserted high school sophomores whose teachers had higher expectations of them were three times more likely to eventually graduate from college than if their teachers had lower expectations of them (Segal, 2014). Higher expectations also relate to academic emphasis, a foundational component of teacher optimism. Thus, the higher expectations that are reported from PCBE schools seem to have a direct, positive correlation with both student engagement and teacher optimism.

"I understand my classes better and then I can do better on the test. It feels GREAT knowing how I will do on a test. And if I mess up, I fix it and can still move on. I like this better, so I'm a lot more motivated. Most of all the kids like it better. They can get ahead, and they have a choice on what to read, and on what to do. It motivates me to move and get done more quickly. It can be harder sometimes to have independence, but I do learn things better. I just have to work harder at it, which is probably a good thing."

—High school student, Idaho

"This is easier to understand why I am learning things and what I need to do. Then I can do better. It makes sense. The standards are easy to understand and I get to say how I will put things together. I'm working harder and doing better than I ever have."

—*Seventh-grade student, California*

A Different View of Grades and Assessment

Third, taking a different view of assessment and grades has a substantial impact on student engagement. Academic success being less dependent on tests and assignments in the PCBE model leads students to believe their progress is more authentic (Ruyle, 2014). Students stress that they better understand why they are learning certain standards, and, therefore, engage more with specific material than they did while "chasing grades" under the traditional system. Martin (2006) noted that the impact of educational interventions aimed at enhancing students' personal bests in terms of their engagement with and achievement on mastery and performance goals over the course of their academic development can be profound. Instruction that focuses on academic growth and personal attainment has the potential to facilitate and increase students' self-efficacy in learning (Bandura, 1997). This is so because, as Martin and Gregory Liem (2010) asserted, "performing as well or better than a previous performance is seen as accessible by students and this perceived accessibility to success enhances students' efficacy regarding their learning" (p. 267). Students in PCBE systems state that since they know exactly what is expected and what proficiency looks like in the performance-based model, they are more confident when taking tests or submitting assessments. Their ability to demonstrate proficiency when they are ready rather than at an arbitrary time set by a teacher is another important factor in their engagement. Teachers we spoke with stressed that appropriate assessments are a critical piece of the performance-based model.

"Here I get to show what I know, and not just get tested on what I don't know. Also, sometimes I might make a mistake, and in the regular class I lose points. A mistake doesn't mean I don't know it—I just made a mistake. I'm always on edge in regular classes."

—*Tenth-grade student, California*

Since learning goals are well defined in the PCBE model, students have a better understanding of the purposes of tasks, enhancing their ability to receive the targeted instruction and assistance they need. In schools that embrace the PCBE model, students can easily describe what success looks like, and why success beyond grades is important for them. In addition, allowing students to demonstrate proficiency when they are ready leads to higher levels of achievement than when using a traditional practice structured around deadlines and test dates. Students know when they are ready to demonstrate proficiency. The fact that they are well aware of what excellence looks like is a motivating factor for them. In practical terms, this means that there is a shift in priorities from simply teaching curriculum and generating grades to focusing on identifying learning goals, creating proficiency scales on those goals that also serve as applied learning progressions, and ensuring that assessments are aligned to the proficiency scales, thereby increasing their reliability and validity. In other words, teachers must take a different view of assessments in that they serve primarily as means to gather information regarding student growth on a continuum of learning. For more detailed discussion on ways to approach alternative grading and assessment, see Marzano (2017), Marzano et al. (2017), and Marzano (2018).

"I took two tests in math this week and got As on both of them. I like being able to go at my own pace and not wait for everybody else. Everybody taking a test in the same day is so silly to me. If I'm ready earlier, why should I have to wait? I have the knowledge, let me go on!"

—*Eleventh-grade student, Montana*

Teacher Proficiency With the PCBE Model

Finally, teachers' ability to implement PCBE structures and practices in the classroom is key to students' experiences. The staff members who fully embrace the PCBE model and connect with students as individuals tend to foster student engagement. On the other end of the spectrum, students express the powerful sentiment that teachers who aren't invested or proficient with PCBE are often the strongest element holding them back from deeper engagement with school. In other words, students are clear that teachers who are not proficient in the PCBE model not only hold them back academically but also contribute to their level of boredom and can reduce their motivation to be successful. Based on our experiences and observations, we would argue that teachers who exhibit a steadfast resolve to cling to the traditional instructional model are extremely frustrating for students.

"I think they need to reteach some of the teachers. They have been doing it the same way for so long that they can't speak to kids in a way that makes sense anymore. They need to be updated so they can teach us and update us in a better way."

—*Ninth-grade student, Ohio*

Implications for Leadership Practice

It is clear that the participation of all stakeholders is critical in energizing evolution and guiding change, as research indicates reforms are more successful when all participants feel ownership and buy-in (Levin, 1999; Stern, 1995). Thus, just as leaders would do well to harness the power of teacher optimism, they must also recognize student engagement as a formidable force in the evolutionary process and an essential component of PCBE. Collaborating with students requires a willingness to listen, share leadership, and be open to shifts in thinking—all of which can make adults wary. Partnering with students does not imply school leaders unilaterally adopt student suggestions but rather implies leaders simply recognize that learners have a perspective they should welcome alongside the wisdom and experience of adult perspectives. When educational leaders find ways to actively solicit student opinions and view students as equal stakeholders in their own learning, schools can better create programs and policies that improve academic achievement.

Among a variety of important practices, five topics are especially salient, and leaders should recognize and cultivate them as powerful strategies to strengthen the student engagement point of the evolutionary triad.

1. Understanding initial student pushback
2. Setting high expectations
3. Communicating learning goals and monitoring student progress with proficiency scales
4. Providing opportunities for student choice
5. Soliciting student voice and involvement in school operations

The following sections discuss each strategy in detail.

Understanding Initial Student Pushback

When introducing the PCBE model of schooling to students, there is often an initial burst of energy and excitement that soon gives way to inevitable pushback. With more student voice and autonomy, students also experience higher expectations and more responsibility. They often respond by wanting to return to what is familiar or rejecting their role in the process. If leaders do not validate the students' feelings, they risk losing the initial momentum. Teachers, who are trying to help students in a model they themselves are not familiar with, may also wish to return to what they know. Leaders must understand and recognize this education model is new for learners, just as it is for teachers. Students are also well aware of what doesn't work in schools, but they have no frame of reference for anything different. Higher expectations in taking responsibility for their own learning will be a challenge for many students who are accustomed to simply following instructions. Telling students school is not about the teaching but rather about the learning is one thing, but it is something different when it happens in reality.

Therefore, it is imperative leaders be clear about reasons for the change and what students can expect. Leaders must be transparent and continually communicate the message of evolution. Keeping students updated regarding the evolutionary process is key. Leaders can accomplish this communication best if they are frequently engaged with the students, walking through classrooms, supporting students with their struggles, and validating their concerns. Further, leaders who are present and engaged with students can help them see that their work and opinions are integral to changing the school system. Students will often get on board before staff, but it remains a new world for them as well. Involving students in creating the school or district vision and mission will validate their input, and celebrating the growth of individuals as well as the larger group will help foster continued positive energy. Understanding and addressing student pushback requires a leader practice mindful leadership by displaying empathy as well as extreme ownership to keep spirits up and the overall mission at the forefront.

Setting High Expectations

High expectations is an essential aspect of PCBE, though the phrase is in danger of losing all meaning. Virtually everyone in education claims to have high expectations in their classrooms and schools; it has become a buzzword. Yet it is important for school leaders to deeply believe all students can learn, instill that belief in all staff members, clearly articulate those high expectations, and strategize ways to empower students to reach those high levels and beyond. To accomplish this, it is important for principals to reinforce that each data point is a learner—a real person—and not just a statistic. Leaders should use data to plan short- and long-term goals, guide teachers' work with students, and enable students to take ownership of their achievement. High expectations are real and powerful and lead to a culture of achievement and collaboration.

Communicating Learning Goals and Monitoring Student Progress With Proficiency Scales

Higher levels of engagement and achievement occur as a result of the organizational and cultural shift in which learning goals, proficiency scales, and aligned assessments become the operating norm. These concepts make expectations explicit; students understand exactly what they are expected to know and be able to do. Strong et al. (1995) addressed the importance of communicating learning goals by stating three important ideas that lead directly to higher levels of engagement:

> 1. *We must clearly articulate the criteria for success and provide clear, immediate, and constructive feedback.*
> 2. *We must show students that the skills they need to be successful are within their grasp by clearly and systematically modeling these skills.*
> 3. *We must help them see success as a valuable aspect of their personalities. (p. 10)*

Marzano (2017) analyzed these concepts at an even deeper level in *The New Art and Science of Teaching* and asserted using proficiency scales to provide and communicate clear learning goals and track student progress is the first element of effective instruction. The process of identifying clear learning goals helps determine the guaranteed and viable curriculum—what learners will master in the instructional time available. Well-designed proficiency scales provide clear focus for instruction of identified learning goals, and the effect on the learners can be powerful because if used correctly, all instructional activities will make sense to them. A proficiency scale brings often esoteric standards to life because students can easily see their goals and their progress.

Assessments also become more relevant when aligned with proficiency scales. Instead of isolated tests given for the purpose of assigning grades, assessments become a feedback loop showing a student's current status and enabling further progress toward a learning goal. Students can see what they need to do next, and teachers can see how to adjust instruction. Learning goals and proficiency scales create a learning-focused system that engages students by giving them clear expectations and agency to reach those goals. See chapter 1 (page 9) for a discussion of the structural design of proficiency scales and to access examples and recommended resources for further reading on developing and implementing these tools.

In addition, educators can measure student engagement using student interviews as well as through quantitative survey tools such as the Panorama Student Survey (PSS; Panorama Education, 2015). Harvard Graduate School of Education researchers designed the PSS (Gehlbach & Brinkworth, 2011) to help schools make more informed decisions about their professional development needs and areas of growth in relation to student needs and engagement. The PSS consists of groups of questions that measure such constructs as engagement, grit, class rigor, relationships, climate, and students' perception of the instructional effectiveness of their teachers. Visit http://panoramaed.com/panorama-student-survey to access all PSS survey questions. Examples of questions include (Panorama Education, 2015):

- *How often do your teachers seem excited to be teaching your classes?*
- *How positive or negative is the energy of your classes?*
- *How often do you get so focused on class activities that you lose track of time?*
- *If you came back to visit class three years from now, how many of your teachers would be excited to see you?*

Providing Opportunities for Student Choice

The most dramatic difference between traditional education and the PCBE model is that traditional settings tend to be curriculum driven and teacher centered. PCBE systems are learner centered, and the curriculum serves as a vehicle to help students move to proficiency on critical learning goals or identified priority standards. As such, student voice and choice is essential in PCBE, and students have the ability, and are encouraged, to display their knowledge and abilities in a variety of ways such as tests and quizzes, presentations, single- or multidisciplinary projects, and probing discussions. It's important for leaders to provide opportunities for learners to accelerate through content and encourage various ways for students to demonstrate their skills and knowledge. Rather than assessments being imposed on students, students have voice and choice in determining how they will demonstrate their abilities. This allows for students to master content in a personally relevant yet rigorous manner.

In the PCBE model, the learner is the agent, and the learning goal is the nucleus the system is designed around. As researcher, educator, and author Bela H. Banathy (1991) asserted, "When learning is in focus, the learner is the actor and the teacher becomes the manager of learning resources" (p. 101). The critical point is how leaders' direct actions have tremendous impact and the potential to empower students with opportunities to fully engage in their learning and their community.

Soliciting Student Voice and Involvement in School Operations

Parker J. Palmer (2007), founder and senior partner emeritus of the Center for Courage and Renewal, writer, speaker, and education activist, asserted that involving students in school operations is an underutilized strategy to increase student engagement:

> *We can offer a curriculum that prepares students to be change agents in some other place at some other time. But if the hidden curriculum of the program simultaneously says, "Don't mess with us!" the lesson our students learn is to stay safe by keeping quiet. When students spend year after year as passive recipients of education, small wonder that they carry their passivity into the workplace. They have not learned, because we did not teach them, that opening one's mouth to challenge what is wrong is a way to stay sane, honor their own integrity, and live by their deepest callings. (p. 11)*

Teachers creating learning spaces that value students' voices and autonomy lead to greater student engagement (Reyes, Brackett, Rivers, White, & Salovey, 2012; Skinner et al., 2008). By extension, the same concept applies to the school as a whole when the adult stakeholders are vigilant in constantly eliciting student involvement in school operations. It is imperative for leaders to create an environment where students are encouraged to challenge and critique academic programs.

For example, professional development and academic direction are almost always the exclusive domain of adult educators in school buildings. Mary Katharine Woodworth, professor of education at Bryn Mawr College, and director of the Teaching and Learning Institute at Bryn Mawr and Haverford Colleges Alison Cook-Sather (2002b) pointed out that, from the earliest days of the educational system, the structure itself (as well as every reform effort) has been premised on the ideals and practice of grown-ups. This practice is not necessarily improper, as the adults are supposed to be the experts in the field of learning and instruction. However, educators who favor student compliance over students truly owning the learning process suppress student engagement and diversity of thought (Apple & Beane, 1995; Fine & Burns, 2003; Sands, Guzman, Stephens, & Boggs, 2007). If educational evolution is to positively impact student achievement, then understanding and responding to students' experiences is essential.

Actively engaging students and honoring their views about what would improve their performance or inspire them to put forth more effort in school will reveal profound insight not previously considered and reinform educational discussions that could advance educational practice. Helping students voice their views not only makes sense for their academic, personal, and behavioral development but also is grounded in cognitive psychology research and critical pedagogies and promotes the underlying social justice goals and values of democracy (Apple & Beane, 1995).

It is important for leaders to welcome student opinions that encompass academics, discipline, and school culture. Although there are a number of ways to engage students in the evolutionary process, four especially pertinent strategies include the following.

1. Use a variety of methods to seek feedback from learners.
2. Seek student voice in a variety of processes.
3. Include student voice in leadership decision making.
4. Partner with students in instructional decisions.

Use a Variety of Methods to Seek Feedback From Learners

Research tools such as surveys are excellent methods that building leaders can use to gather schoolwide data regarding a host of student perception issues such as bullying, engagement, academic rigor, and pedagogical effectiveness. One example is the Panorama Student Survey, which can gauge feedback from students in a variety of areas.

Another useful practice is for leaders to use brief conversations with and observations of learners to gather quick data on students' opinions and feelings regarding school policies and culture, what's happening in the hallways and common areas, and the content and structure of their classes. Leaders should also seek the partnership of students by asking for feedback on what's working in their classes as part of teacher evaluations. This is not to say students have power over personnel decisions, but maintaining a focus on learners in the classroom is a more powerful and effective strategy for improving instruction than simply monitoring instructional methods.

Seek Student Voice in a Variety of Processes

In addition to collecting ideas and data from and about students, educational leaders can actually teach students the processes of collecting and analyzing information and collaborating to solve problems. For example, leaders and teachers can teach students to help look at and process survey and interview data. Also, when administrators present budgetary issues to teacher groups for their consideration, they should likewise consult student groups for their feedback. At the secondary level, this could entail discussing the economic realities in mathematics, business, or social studies classes, or conducting a survey to find out students' opinions about district budget priorities. At the elementary level, age-appropriate surveys are also an effective strategy, as are interviews to discern student ideas and opinions regarding what is working or not working for them in school. Presenting budget issues to students demonstrates transparency and ethical leadership, treats students as equal stakeholders in their own education, and honors the ability of learners to serve as problem solvers. In fact, students' insights that generate ideas to save or redistribute monies can be profound. In our experience, many adults assume operating this way slows the process because students will only speak from a self-centered agenda, but authentically involving them in solving issues the school faces can lead to increased understanding and buy-in, as well as profound and invaluable perspectives.

Include Student Voice in Leadership Decision Making

Principals should consciously carve out space for students to provide input through participation on school leadership teams, school improvement teams, or any other committees that impact students directly. It is important these committees regard students as full members, not just observers. Students' feedback must receive due respect.

At the elementary level, leaders could include student voice by interviewing students about their classroom experiences or working with student teams to create and communicate the school vision. In middle and high school, strategies could include the following.

- Evaluating curriculum, teachers, or classes
- Analyzing school climate, culture, perceptions, and spirit
- Joining school improvement committees as full members
- Co-creating classroom norms and outcomes for behavior

Additionally, schools can include students in the hiring process for new staff, perhaps even participating in teacher and building leader interviews. This can provide tremendous energy and does not diminish the level of professionalism in that critical process. Participation actually teaches students how to operate in real-world settings and demonstrates to potential future staff that the school values and respects student voice.

Partner With Students in Instructional Decisions

Even many traditional schools expect students to participate in meetings regarding their individualized education plans (IEPs). PCBE systems should take this partnership in instructional decisions to the next level. Individual students should be included in any discussion that directly affects them, such as parent-teacher conferences, student support meetings, and so on. When school leaders set new goals or make a major decision, they should expect students to contribute. At the same time, educators should be willing to help students as they shape and achieve their own aspirations for learning.

When schools provide opportunities to increase student agency, the results can be transformational. The process of becoming engaged as active partners can give young people a broader perspective and provide strategies they can use to create positive change in their future classrooms, workplaces, or communities. The school as a whole benefits as well. Reform efforts initiated with student input are more likely to be successful in the long term and improve the learning environment for all students (Cook-Sather, 2002a, 2002c). When adults demonstrate appreciation and respect for learners, students will typically feel more connected to their school community, which can foster deep, lasting bonds that extend beyond the school day.

Effective educational evolution must necessarily include the voice of students, because, as Cook-Sather (2002a) noted:

> *As long as we exclude [student] perspectives from our conversations about schooling and how it needs to change, our efforts at reform will be based on an incomplete picture of life in classrooms and schools and how that life could be improved. (p. 3)*

Soliciting and placing a high value on student voice powerfully contributes to educational evolution, and the tremendous potential impact of student voice in schools demands leaders who are willing to listen and carry out change. Students are the experts on what works for them, and educators ignore students' perceptions at their own peril.

Summary

Critical scholar and expert consultant John Smyth (2006) asserted:

> *When students feel that their lives, experiences, cultures, and aspirations are ignored, trivialized, or denigrated, they develop a hostility to the institution of schooling. They feel that schooling is simply not worth the emotional and psychological investment necessary to warrant their serious involvement. (p. 285)*

Motivation and engagement are not simply "feel good" concepts that matter little in classrooms or are beyond the scope of teacher responsibility. Engagement results in higher levels of student effort, interest, and attention; mindful and constructive student participation; and motivation for deliberate practice, ultimately providing the opportunity for learners to improve their academic skills and build confidence (Fredricks, Blumenfeld, & Paris, 2004; Marks, 2000; Reyes et al., 2012; Skinner & Belmont, 1993). Our experience in schools reflects that when educators partner with students to improve learning, teaching, and leadership in schools, the changes are positive and effective. Engaged students can have a tremendous impact on the overall evolution of a school—in fact, without student impact, initiatives are bound to fail. By redesigning educational systems, schools can move from reactive to proactive mode, and begin to examine and undertake the much more fundamental changes necessary to engage all students in deeper and productive learning.

CHAPTER 5

The High-Impact School

Should you find yourself in a chronically leaking boat, energy devoted to changing vessels is more productive than energy devoted to patching leaks.

—Warren Buffett

In systems that succeed in transforming to the PCBE model with the evolutionary triad at the center, leaders invite their greatest resources—the teachers—to imagine a system that allows their ideals and goals to become a living, working reality. This is what is known as a *high-impact school.* Leaders and teachers together become learners, dreamers, and innovators. Then they invite the other stakeholders—the students, their parents, and the community—to create a vision of excellence for their school and the learning that will take place there. With this clear direction, all parts of the evolutionary triad stand together, focus their effort toward the vision, and push forward.

The initial transformation may be small and might go unnoticed. Some may even lose heart or want to retreat because the effort is not producing tangible results fast enough. But the leader persists, reminding the rest of the triad they are all capable together, providing new resources, and modeling a growth mindset. The leader helps a teacher team develop collective efficacy, a teacher connects with a student about his or her aspirations for learning beyond school, and an individual student realizes he or she *can* learn without the constraints of a traditional classroom.

Support from leadership bolsters the teachers to empower students and impact their learning. Teachers dig deep; they persevere because they believe their efforts will make a difference. Students see and feel the efforts of the adults and know their own experiences matter in the system, so they re-engage. The system changes.

Momentum builds with each success. The practice of continuous improvement through the involvement of all three parts of the triad becomes the norm. The massive educational bureaucracy is forced to evolve to support individual learning. The institutional constraints from bygone eras fall away, replaced with innovative structures that support individual learning. Stagnant, lackluster performance gives way as individuals are empowered through their own learning and personal growth. The system changes and keeps moving forward with the people whose efforts started it moving in the first place.

It is imperative for stakeholders in these schools to not take this momentum for granted. They must actively work to sustain and improve their evolution once they succeed in transforming their school or district. In this chapter, we'll look at the ways leaders can ensure they continue to strengthen the PCBE system in their school or district and monitor evolutionary growth to ensure its continued success.

Strengthen the System

When instructional leaders who transform schools consciously attend to teacher optimism and student engagement—and when the evolutionary triad is fully functional—these leaders can take their schools to the next level. In the following sections, we explore some of the practical growth areas, such as supportive structures and practices to sustain and nurture the evolutionary triad long term. In order to maintain the triad's momentum, it is important to continuously monitor the systems by creating High Reliability Schools, cultivating relationships with supportive outside institutions, and shifting hiring and training priorities to ensure the best cultural match with people who will eventually join the team.

Creating High Reliability Schools

Instructional leaders who transform schools can learn from other types of successful organizational structures. High reliability organizations continually pursue top performance. Examples of high reliability organizations include airplane maintenance companies and nuclear power plants. Employees of these organizations must constantly monitor for errors in critical factors, immediately take action to keep those errors from becoming systemwide failures, and recognize the interrelatedness of their operation systems. It is interesting to note that, for much of the 20th and 21st centuries, schools have not typically been part of the high reliability organization conversation and have been willing to accept high levels of failure (Marzano et al., 2014). In response to this phenomenon, Marzano, Warrick, and Simms (2014) analyzed contemporary research from the business field and created a framework for helping evolve schools into high reliability organizations. When executed well, the High Reliability Schools (HRS) framework results in improved educational systems and ensures leaders can positively impact all components of the evolutionary triad.

Marzano, Warrick, and Simms (2014) outlined five levels of operation for High Reliability Schools in their High Reliability Schools framework, synthesized from Hattie's (2009, 2012) top fifty factors influencing student achievement: (1) safe and collaborative culture, (2) effective teaching in every classroom, (3) guaranteed and viable curriculum, (4) standards-referenced reporting, and (5) competency-based education. These are the conditions associated with successful schools and continual school improvement.

First, achieving a safe and collaborative culture requires the entire educational organization to function as a PLC, which DuFour et al. (2016) describe as "an ongoing process in which educators work collaboratively in recurring cycles of collective inquiry and action research to achieve better results for the students they serve" (p. 10). Ensuring such a culture is the foundational level of the HRS framework. Within the larger school organization, grade-level or departmental collaborative teams consider and discuss the fundamental work of improving teaching and learning. It is the responsibility of the leader to create the best possible conditions for collaborative teams to function and thrive.

As noted in chapter 2 (page 31), there are four critical questions at the heart of PLC work (DuFour et al., 2008, 2016; DuFour & Eaker, 1998).

1. What knowledge, skills, and dispositions should every student acquire as a result of the unit, course, or grade level?
2. How will we know when each student has acquired the essential knowledge and skills?
3. How will we respond when some students do not learn?
4. How will we extend the learning for students who are already proficient?

Additionally, three big ideas drive the work of a PLC: (1) a focus on learning, (2) a collaborative culture and collective responsibility, and (3) a results orientation. In a PLC, collaborative teams regularly interact to address common issues regarding curriculum, instruction, assessment, and student academic achievement. The PLC process provides training, support, and collaboration and is critical for practicing and deepening instructional strategies among all teachers. To learn more about the PLC process and to support your work toward creating a safe and collaborative culture, see DuFour et al. (2016) and Marzano, Heflebower, Hoegh, Warrick, and Grift (2016).

Second, because a teacher's effectiveness is the single most important factor for schools in increasing student achievement, a system should exist to provide teachers with feedback and an accurate and credible measurement of their individual instructional performances. The primary purpose should be teacher development, and instructional leaders should respond to information gleaned from these evaluations with focused, powerful training sessions. Two of the most popular and powerful evaluation tools are the Danielson Framework for Teaching Evaluation Instrument and the Marzano Focused Teacher Evaluation Model. Visit www.danielsongroup.org/framework and www.marzanocenter.com/Teacher-Evaluation respectively to learn more about these methods.

Third, school leaders should continually monitor the viability of the guaranteed curriculum and its effect on student achievement. Ways to achieve this include training and assisting teachers in communicating clear learning goals, developing aligned proficiency scales, and charting learner progress toward those learning goals through valid and reliable assessment practices. Refer to Marzano (2017) as a guide for this work.

Fourth, the grading and reporting systems must align with the teacher-identified learning goals and proficiency scales. When schools make this shift, teachers score assignments and assessments based on the relevant proficiency scale. Traditional omnibus grades on the A–F or 100-point scales are abandoned in favor of report cards showing students' status and growth toward learning goals. To support such a shift in grading systems, refer to Marzano (2010) and Heflebower, Hoegh, and Warrick (2014).

Finally, a fully realized High Reliability School abolishes time constraints by creating a PCBE system that allows learners to move through systems of knowledge at varied rates. In schools where this has become common practice, there is a corresponding increase in academic optimism and student engagement, both having a direct correlation to subsequent student achievement. For guidance in creating a system that allows students to work at their own pace, refer to Lindsay Unified School District (2017); Schwahn and McGarvey (2012, 2014); Daggett and McNulty (2010); DeLorenzo, Battino, Schreiber, and Carrio (2009); and Marzano, Norford, Finn, and Finn (2017).

Visit **www.MarzanoResources.com/hrs** to find additional information on the Marzano High Reliability Schools (HRS) framework. While the evolutionary triad is a key framework for leaders to ensure practices are having positive effects on stakeholders, the HRS framework defines schoolwide structures that help build toward a complete PCBE system.

Cultivating Relationships With Outside Institutions

Just as schools and districts find it challenging to evolve to new educational paradigms, many institutions of higher education suffer the same fate. A common refrain from numerous college education departments regarding real innovation revolves around the faculty's perceived responsibility to prepare educators to work in traditional schools. Most schools of education do not offer robust curriculum in systems design for future educational models. This perpetuates a lack of understanding of innovative systems—what they look like and how to prepare teachers and administrators to lead new paradigms. To realize evolutionary change, we need educational leaders with understanding and skills in this area. A powerful leadership strategy for evolution entails leaders contacting various other agencies and establishing partnerships.

Around the world, there are also university faculty working to develop innovative classroom lessons, discover effective instructional practices, and bring theory to life in real schools. In addition, researchers in labs and think tanks are often developing new resources and tools and seeking to test new educational technologies. To find and connect with such researchers, good resources to consult include Learning Sciences International (www.learningsciences.com) and the International Association for K–12 Online Learning (iNACOL; https://inacol.org).

By partnering with local universities, teachers might receive new curriculum or access new technology to enhance content-area learning. In addition, these partnerships can help teach college professors about the new model and get them back into the field on a practical, real-life level. It can be a positive scenario for both sides when schools gain insight from research and university faculty are better able to start preparing teachers and leaders for the changes.

Furthermore, reaching out to innovative organizations such as KnowledgeWorks, Education Reimagined, and CompetencyWorks, as well as schools that have successfully implemented (or even attempted but failed to implement) PCBE systems, can provide a wealth of information and guidance (visit https://knowledgeworks.org, https://education-reimagined.org, and www.competencyworks.org respectively for more information about these organizations). Connecting with schools involved in implementing the PCBE model could provide a wealth of information and new educational colleagues with whom to engage. Some of the leading PCBE schools readers may benefit from connecting with include Mesa County Valley School District 51 in Grand Junction, Colorado (www.d51schools.org), Lindsay Unified School District in California (www.lindsay.k12.ca.us), Highland Academy Charter School in Anchorage, Alaska (www.asdk12.org/domain/3191), and Regional School Unit 2 in the Kennebec Intra-District Schools in Hallowell, Maine (www.kidsrsu.org). Research-based professional development companies provide experienced professionals to work directly with teachers in their classrooms, and the U.S. Department of Education's Regional Education Laboratories (RELs; see https://ies.ed.gov/ncee/edlabs) help make research accessible.

Partnerships with colleges and innovative agencies provide a powerful connection to evolving schools because they fulfill short-term needs, such as training new teachers to enter the field ready for innovation, and long-term needs, such as sustaining innovation over time. Partnerships are empowering to teachers because they give them a voice in the system preparing their future colleagues, engage them in professional dialogue, and break the isolation of traditional settings. Partnerships also create opportunities to study the impact of the innovation on student learning and to sustain continuous improvement. In addition, forging partnerships with innovative organizations is a way to bring people together so they can help and learn from each other. This makes education a fast-paced field for the first time ever.

Shifting Hiring and Training Priorities

Hiring and job placement decisions have the potential to seriously impact teacher teams and students for years. To cultivate higher teacher optimism and student engagement, it is critical to build a faculty with people who demonstrate certain qualities such as the ability to collaborate, be vulnerable, and be open to growth; a teachable spirit; a moral purpose for educating all learners; and a focus on equity and excellence. We've noticed a tendency for schools to focus on a cookie-cutter screening and interview process that really only tests how well an applicant does under certain artificial circumstances; it is not the customized process it should be. For example, through our collective school experience, we have seen that school leaders often place a very high value on classroom experience when hiring new teachers. Indeed, experience can be a valuable trait and may be a good indicator of subsequent success. However, experience can blind administrators and hiring committees to equally valuable professional and personal qualities such as open-mindedness and willingness to collaborate.

In fact, Development Dimensions International (DDI), a global training company, published its High-Resolution Leadership report in 2015, which sought to determine the most important job skills required by 2020. The study of over fifteen thousand leaders in over three hundred organizations across twenty industries and eighteen countries identified *empathy* as the most critical driver of overall performance (Sinar, Wellins, Paese, Smith, & Watt, 2016). Additionally, the researchers asserted emotional intelligence an important predictor of job success, even surpassing technical ability, high IQ, and experience (Sinar et al., 2016). Based on these findings (Sinar et al., 2016), it is advisable for principals of effective PCBE schools to focus beyond content knowledge. If a teacher's job is not to *teach* students, but rather to help students *learn*, leaders should attempt to build a faculty around more relevant qualities such as empathy, flexibility, and a candidate's ability to alter practice for the benefit of all learners.

Instructional leaders who transform schools surround themselves with people who are amenable to change and take advantage of every opportunity to help during a transition. Effective PCBE leaders hire teachers with the flexibility to deal with uncertain and unpredictable situations. They seek teachers who feel a sense of responsibility and ownership to step into the fray and try to solve problems. These leaders also seek emergent leaders who can sustain safe, fair environments. They hire empathetic teachers who think about their students' and their colleagues' lives, understand their challenges and frustrations, and know those emotions are every bit as real as their own.

In addition, strengthening post-hiring practices such as mentorship, reflection, observation, and evaluation to support new hires can aid in retention of high-quality staff members. Many teachers might be willing to commit to the new system, but they may quickly become overwhelmed if schools don't have structures in place to support them. In effective PCBE organizations, teacher productivity is very high, student engagement is high, and leadership is innovative. Top candidates flock to these organizations and are not as apt to leave them.

Addressing the needs of various ethnic groups is also an important topic for leaders to consider during the hiring process and beyond. In addition to a conscious and concerted effort to hire and train a more diverse pool of teachers and leaders, subsequent professional development is an equally important component for continued growth. Ongoing training and professional development is necessary to focus on the teacher qualities discussed in this section. Some schools are able to tap into local resources in order to meet this need, but there are numerous examples of exceptionally well-trained and seasoned experts schools can access online. For example, San Diego State University professor of education J. Luke Wood, an expert on the education of men and boys of color, created a free online class called Black Minds Matter that addresses how educators and administrators can work against the disparities facing students of color by focusing on effective principles of practice. This course helps teachers apply these principles in a real-life context to try to reach students and change the paradigm that they encounter. Visit https://jlukewood.com/black-minds-matter for more information about this course. Additionally, the organization Epoch Education provides a wide variety of training and resources to address issues of diversity, inherent bias, and effective cultural practices. Visit https://epocheducation.com for more information about the resources Epoch offers.

"When the administration . . . hires people here, they look for 'fit,' not just certification. I've been through lots of interviews before and was never asked questions like I was in the interview here. It's unique. Not a single question about my content knowledge, but they were probing to see how open-minded I would be and how adaptable to a new way of doing business. And if someone doesn't fit, they don't just hammer them, but they try to help them find a job elsewhere that could be a better match for them. The change is happening and most of us have fully bought in here."

—High school teacher, California

Monitor Evolutionary Growth

When shifting to a new model of education, it is important to note typical methods of gauging success are not always immediately clear. Student scores on standardized tests will not necessarily rise dramatically in the early stages of implementing a new educational system. In fact, they may initially drop slightly due to the implementation dip common to new initiatives. This reality often fuels the opposition to moving away from traditional pedagogy. However, data suggest that scores on standardized tests that measure higher levels of student achievement will ultimately rise in the PCBE model as students demonstrate true proficiency on the standards (Anderson, 2014; Ruyle, 2014). Also, if the PCBE system is implemented and nurtured through strong and effective leadership, schools will witness higher levels of teacher optimism and student engagement—both having a direct correlation with subsequent higher student achievement.

It is critical for leaders to document the progress schools make during the evolution process, and the best way to do that is through constant evaluation. In a classroom, frequent assessment and timely student growth data are critical to instruction and progress toward a learning goal. Likewise, monitoring schoolwide growth statistics is also central to successful implementation of an initiative or innovation. Far too often in education, new initiatives are mandated and implemented with no defined way to track progress or to chart whether the new idea actually works. Thus, efforts to analyze long-term trends are often hampered by a lack of good data. There is a critical need to see how schooling is affecting current students and to make immediate adjustments in the classroom. Monitoring and evaluating is an essential leadership behavior (Marzano et al., 2005) and speaks to the importance of creating a system that provides feedback about growth toward identified goals. Ideally, the system will be designed to continually monitor the school's curriculum, instruction, and assessment practices, as well as the impact of those practices on student achievement. In the following sections, we will examine types of data; methods for collecting, sharing, and analyzing the data; and the importance of celebrating accomplishments when the data indicate growth.

Formal Data

Although charting the effectiveness of the PCBE model can be exceedingly difficult using traditional measures, the concepts of teacher optimism and student engagement provide a compelling means to monitor progress. It is possible to project reliable full-year academic statistics by monitoring growth in teacher optimism and student engagement—both of which have a direct correlation to student achievement. The projection necessarily assumes that innovations that impact the student engagement–teacher optimism bottom line are continuing to evolve and result in better teaching and learning.

Leaders can use the School Academic Optimism Scale (SAOS) to gather formal data to monitor teacher optimism. The Ohio State University Fawcett professor emeritus Wayne Hoy (2005) designed the SAOS to measure teacher beliefs and attitudes related to self-efficacy, faculty trust in students and parents, and the academic focus of the school. Visit http://waynekhoy.com/pdfs/saos.pdf to access the complete survey. The survey contains thirty statements for respondents to rate, such as (Hoy, 2005):

- *Teachers here are confident they will be able to motivate their students.*
- *Teachers in this school believe that every child can learn.*
- *Academic achievement is recognized and acknowledged by the school.*
- *Students try hard to improve on previous work.*

Combine the three areas of (1) collective efficacy, (2) trust, and (3) academic emphasis to create an overall academic optimism score educators can use to compare schools or districts to the normal distribution, as shown in table 5.1.

Table 5.1: SAOS Score Distribution

SAOS Score	Distribution
800	Higher than 99 percent of schools
700	Higher than 97 percent of schools
600	Higher than 84 percent of schools
500	Average
400	Lower than 84 percent of schools
300	Lower than 97 percent of schools
200	Lower than 99 percent of schools

Source: Hoy, 2015.

Consider the following excerpt from a conversation we had with one district-level leader who employed the SAOS to gain data regarding teacher attitudes toward the educational culture in the district. This leader describes the benefit his school district experienced from continually monitoring its progress in implementing the PCBE model using SAOS data.

"It was an easy process. We started by recreating the survey as a Google form and administered the survey to all of our teachers during a professional development day in January. In less than twenty minutes, principals were able to collect data that provided them with some interesting insight into their building culture. We really like how the survey returned scores for each of the three areas [collective efficacy, trust, and academic emphasis] as well as the overall academic optimism score. We were a little surprised by some of the results, both positive and negative, but it has given us a deeper understanding of interrelatedness of building culture and PCBE.

"The first way we looked at the data was through the lens of the overall academic optimism score. This overall score gave us a way to compare each building to the average school as well as comparing the level of academic optimism to the level of PCBE implementation. As we expected, those schools that were further along in implementation demonstrated levels of academic optimism significantly above the national average.

"Next, we looked at our scores from the three individual components of the SAOS: collective efficacy, faculty trust in parents and teachers, and the academic emphasis of the school. We could see distinct breaks in the data between elementary and secondary schools in all three areas. Our elementary schools reported higher scores on each component than did our secondary schools, which correlated with the level of PCBE implementation as well as performance on state exams.

"Culture can be one of those tricky things to gather data on. We know it is essential for change, and even more so for the shift to PCBE. The SAOS provided us with a quick and simple tool to focus our work by identifying strengths and weaknesses in our culture."

—*Administrator, Missouri*

In addition to the SAOS, educational leaders can use student interviews and the Panorama Student Survey (PSS; Panorama Education, 2015) to gather formal data that measure student engagement. See chapter 4 (page 85) for a deeper discussion of the PSS.

Using formal data collection protocols lends credibility to an initiative and allows an educational leader to paint a more vivid picture of the results of implementing an innovation such as PCBE. Formal data also allow a leader to address the urgent need to continue implementation efforts in the most compelling way. The SAOS and PSS are both valid, reliable, and scientifically designed tools that directly speak to two of the three points of the evolutionary triad: teacher optimism and student engagement. As powerful as the data from these tools are, however, adding informal data allows a leader to tell an even more robust story that can be compelling to all stakeholders.

Informal Data

Teachers and administrators should also use quick conversations and observations to collect data that will allow them to analyze their progress on their evolutionary journey, hone their practice working with data, and chart the effectiveness of identified interventions. Educators can use classroom observations to gauge pedagogical effectiveness by gathering data on the application of effective instructional practice and impact on engagement. Asking questions of students and teachers can serve as mini-interviews that provide information about the effectiveness of the overall program. Author and University of Nebraska–Lincoln professor of educational psychology John Creswell (2003) described interviews as "qualitative research procedures for describing, analyzing, and interpreting a culture-sharing group's shared patterns of behavior, beliefs, and language that develop over time" (p. 14). Talking to students and teachers regularly during the day allows for the exploration of culture and shared beliefs among people in the school. Customize questions such as the following to ascertain pertinent, powerful information quickly.

- What are your learning goals? Do you know why you do what you do in class?
- Can you describe how what you learn in school is valuable and relevant to your life?
- How do you engage and motivate students?
- Are the academic expectations here at a high level? Can you give an example of how you can take all students to a higher level?

Ultimately, gathering quick, informal data gleaned from student and teacher discussions provides qualitative evidence that can be combined with the results of more formal assessments like the SAOS and PSS to paint a richer picture of student engagement and teacher optimism.

Student Achievement Data

Monitoring growth in a number of facets is critical in leading the evolution of schools. Thus, in addition to charting the increase of teacher optimism and student engagement to gather information for planning and executing positive change, monitoring student achievement is also important. As mentioned previously, infrequent data sources such as statewide assessments are somewhat limited as measures of progress. PCBE systems use frequent classroom assessments to track individual student achievement on learning goals, class growth, and school progress. Increasingly, schools are using software programs to collect and analyze these data. Unfortunately, the vast majority of the commercially available programs, such as PowerSchool (www.powerschool.com), Infinite Campus (www.infinitecampus.com), and Aeries (www.aeries.com), are designed to appeal to schools still practicing traditional education models. Although these programs often claim to have standards-based components built into their technology, few are particularly user friendly or meet the needs of schools and districts truly evolving to a PCBE model. In fact, these traditional progress-monitoring systems are among the biggest factors limiting educational evolution because they maintain focus on traditional grading—school teams find their technological capabilities inhibiting. In contrast, one monitoring system I have used, Empower Learning, is the first PCBE educator-developed, comprehensive learning management system specifically designed to support the PCBE model. Visit https://empowerlearning.net for information about the Empower Learning system.

Transparent Data Sharing and Analysis

It is critical educational leaders present the data collected from surveys, discussions, and interviews in a transparent manner so information flows freely and clearly among all stakeholders. Leaders can accomplish this by sharing the data in staff meetings, posting them on school or district websites, displaying visual presentations of the data on walls in the school, presenting the data at public school board meetings, and sharing them with local media sources. When evolutionary change is occurring, people can often feel it is negatively impacting their established system of order and protocol. In one sense, this is true—this change challenges the system ingrained in U.S. society for more than 150 years. Monitoring progress and communicating the data regularly will assuage fears, demonstrate things are not falling apart, and provide evidence the school is truly making progress.

Continually monitoring the impact of an initiative such as PCBE is important for schools to keep moving forward as well as for the advancement and purposeful reform of education as a whole to occur. Just as in a classroom—where a variety of assessments provide information reflecting a student's growth toward a learning goal—data from surveys, observations, interviews, academic testing, and discipline referrals can paint a rich picture of an organization's growth and evolution. This transparency is important in maintaining momentum inside the building as well as support from stakeholders in the larger community.

"We gathered lots of data during the implementation period. The district posted the data and hired a data specialist. Now is the time to be true to their word and follow through on this. We are working on a system for all kids. That's really important, and I can see it happening now!"

—*Middle school teacher, Washington*

Celebrations

With monitoring processes in place, leaders should also use the resulting information to celebrate growth. Celebrating success and progress during the challenging times of evolving and transforming schools is critical for teacher optimism. As one humorous example, consider the high school principal who presented staff with the idea of the two major contributors to a bacon-and-egg breakfast—although the chicken is *involved*, the pig is *committed*. The principal used the comparison to illustrate the level of commitment necessary to shift to PCBE. The staff embraced the analogy and displayed their commitment to the PCBE system by placing pig posters around the building, distributing pig trinkets as rewards to staff members, and posting pig-themed quotes in weekly briefings. Other schools or teacher teams have referred to themselves as *revolutionaries* or *pioneers* and taken on the persona of famous change agents from the past.

The school should celebrate students and student growth as well. Celebrations create energy to help the organization move through the inevitable difficult periods. Some possibilities include periodic celebrations spotlighting student growth or teacher success, display boards listing positive news prominently posted in the building, partnering with local media outlets to publicize student achievement, or recognizing group accomplishments in community meetings. The key is to transparently celebrate success and challenges, acknowledge risk taking, and authentically keep people informed of progress.

Summary

Effective high-impact PCBE schools are continually evolving in a constant quest to improve student learning to the highest levels possible. In addition to being a haven for teacher optimism and student engagement, PCBE schools become a safe place to innovate, fail, and learn. PCBE schools also become learning communities for all stakeholders in the educational process, able to meet the needs of both students and teachers as they undergo the learning process. Toward this end, it is important schools striving toward the PCBE model consider schoolwide structures such as those in the Marzano High Reliability Schools framework (Marzano et al., 2014). Thus, in high-impact PCBE schools, the collaboration shapes the culture, professional evaluation systems focus on teacher development in the same way teachers focus on student development toward learning goals in the classroom, and learning goals and proficiency scales are accepted norms across the school.

Monitoring growth on numerous measures such as engagement and optimism in addition to student achievement is a hallmark of PCBE schools. Data are transparent, so leaders can acknowledge struggles and areas for growth as well as publicly celebrate success. A variety of tools to chart and present results are available, and data derived from measurement tools become the foundation for future planning of school goals and professional development. PCBE schools also foster a culture in which openness is encouraged and educators actively seek professional collaboration with colleagues, other schools, research agencies, and higher-level educational programs.

EPILOGUE

You never change things by fighting the existing reality. To change something, build a new model that makes the existing model obsolete.

—Buckminster Fuller

Common sense tells us that when students are more engaged with the classroom learning, teachers will be more optimistic. Likewise, when teachers are more positive and optimistic, it creates an environment in which students tend to be more engaged. There is a direct, positive correlation between students' engagement and the academic optimism of their teachers, and this relationship represents a powerful force when used in school evolution. Understanding this fundamental connection provides educational leaders with valuable information to assist them as they lead the evolutionary change required to implement PCBE systems.

Educational reform has been a much-debated topic from the very inception of school systems. University of Colorado education professor Robert Linn (2001) has asserted that the controversy around educational assessment practice began in the 19th century (as cited in Marzano, 2018). In addition, in the early 19th century, Horace Mann, secretary of the Massachusetts State Board of Education, began reforming the state's school system and installing many elements of the traditional model with which we are all too familiar (Mintz & McNeil, 2016), while John Dewey introduced his famous philosophy of educational reform in 1916. Since 2000, these discussions have shifted more toward the issues of charter schools, competition, choice, and vouchers to confront many of the inadequacies of the traditional public school system. However, the tangible results from these movements and a host of other initiatives purporting to ensure higher levels of academic achievement have proven them inconsequential at best and dismal failures at worst. The reason for this disappointing phenomenon is not due to the relative merits of the movements themselves, but rather because of their focus on shortcomings within schools as opposed to on addressing the larger issue—that the entire U.S. educational system has been unable to adapt at the same pace as the rest of the world. Blaming principals, teachers, parents, students, and society while continuing to inadequately fund an antiquated system is certainly a road to disaster—yet U.S. schools often stubbornly remain fixed on the same path. What is needed in schools—in this most critical of organizations—is an evolution of the existing model into one that is more innovative, relevant, effective, and successful.

In order to transform 150 years of tired tradition and educational inertia, great leaders must take extreme ownership of their moral responsibility to evolve schools. It is an honor and a privilege to be in a leadership position in schools. School leaders are responsible for the students in their care, and their key concern is to help ensure each and every child achieves his or her personal best. With this responsibility rests the moral imperative for leaders to cultivate their personal capacity, will, and courage to lead boldly. Leaders and educational experts must necessarily move academic organizations forward. But with real, substantive reform no algorithm exists; it's not clean and easy—it's messy.

Based on our collective experience and research, we assert that when effectively implemented, PCBE systems produce happier students, happier teachers, and outcomes any community would wish for their children and their future. The research clearly indicates the skills and abilities central to leading the change to a PCBE system are coherent vision, empowerment of staff and students, and transformational instructional leadership. Change needs to be systemic, yet focused. It requires school and district leaders with a high tolerance for ambiguity and dissent, a deep commitment to remedy weaknesses in the system, and the ability to inspire others to the same depth of commitment. To initiate and sustain change, leaders "must be able to lead such an endeavor successfully over the long term, despite potential setbacks and the significant work that will be required to make changes in the day-to-day strategies and processes of teachers, administrators, support staff, and the school as a whole" (DeLorenzo et al., 2009, p. 137).

The main goal of this book is to inspire current and future leaders to reflect on professional practice to become instructional leaders who transform schools. The best schools are willing to disrupt the status quo to become innovative, proactive educational organizations. As such, future leaders must view students and teachers as equally important—parts of a three-pronged approach to evolutionary growth. Teachers need solid direction, effective coaching, permission to take risks, and time to practice new skills and adjust based on feedback. Students need clear learning goals, road maps pointing them toward proficiency, feedback regarding their growth, and personal support to achieve their highest potential. Ultimately, teachers, students, and leaders all need time to study, discuss, practice, and evolve their learning. They need continued support.

Educational evolution is not a grassroots process. Stakeholders must be brought on board, but teachers, students, and communities will only evolve if quality programs are led from the top. Leaders must consciously cultivate the kind of organizational processes that strengthen and support the abilities of all. Leaders must empower students and teachers by defining the mission and goals with them, and then facilitate collaboration so everyone can learn together. Schools need people to be emotionally involved in the process, take courageous steps, and lead from the front. Leaders must be vigilant and fiercely protect the bottom line of the evolutionary triad—the teacher optimism–student engagement connection that forms the very foundation of effective education. The ultimate mission for educational leaders is to embrace and act on the words of Martin Luther King Jr. (2010):

> *Human progress is neither automatic nor inevitable. Even a superficial look at history reveals that no social advance rolls in on the wheels of inevitability. Every step towards the goal of justice requires sacrifice, suffering, and struggle; the tireless exertions and passionate concern of dedicated individuals. Without persistent effort, time itself becomes an ally of the insurgent and primitive forces of irrational emotionalism and social destruction. This is no time for apathy or complacency. This is a time for vigorous and positive action. (p. 191)*

REFERENCES AND RESOURCES

ACT. (2016). *Profile report—national: Graduating class of 2016.* Accessed at www.act.org/content/dam/act/unsecured/documents/P_99_999999_N_S_N00_ACT-GCPR_National.pdf on January 19, 2018.

Alexander, K. L., Entwisle, D. R., & Horsey, C. S. (1997). From first grade forward: Early foundations of high school dropout. *Sociology of Education, 70*(2), 87–107.

Allegretto, S. A., & Mishel, L. (2016). The teacher pay gap is wider than ever. *Economic Policy Institute.* Accessed at www.epi.org/publication/the-teacher-pay-gap-is-wider-than-ever-teachers-pay-continues-to-fall-further-behind-pay-of-comparable-workers on May 29, 2018.

Altenbaugh, R. J. (Ed.). (1999). *Historical dictionary of American education.* Westport, CT: Greenwood Press.

Anderson, T. J. (2014). *Transforming educational paradigms: A case study of two different schools on the path toward implementing personalized mastery practices* (Doctoral dissertation). Montana State University, Bozeman. Accessed at https://scholarworks.montana.edu/xmlui/bitstream/handle/1/8767/AndersonT1214.pdf on January 19, 2018.

Andrews, R. L., Basom, M. R., & Basom, M. (1991). Instructional leadership: Supervision that makes a difference. *Theory Into Practice, 30*(2), 97–101.

Annamma, S. A., Boelé, A. L., Moore, B. A., & Klingner, J. (2013). Challenging the ideology of normal in schools. *International Journal of Inclusive Education, 17*(12), 1278–1294.

Apple, M. W., & Beane, J. A. (Eds.). (1995). *Democratic schools.* Alexandria, VA: Association for Supervision and Curriculum Development.

Appleton, J., Christenson, S., & Furlong, M. (2008). Student engagement with school: Critical conceptual and methodological issues of the construct. *Psychology in the Schools, 45*(5), 369–386.

Arkansas Department of Education. (2014). *Professional development.* Accessed at www.arkansased.gov/divisions/learning-services/professional-development on June 12, 2018.

Audas, R., & Willms, J. D. (2001). *Engagement and dropping out of school: A life-course perspective.* Hull, Quebec, Canada: Applied Research Branch, Strategic Policy, Human Resources Development Canada.

Baker, B. D. (2016). *Does money matter in education?* (2nd ed.). Washington, DC: Albert Shanker Institute. Accessed at www.shankerinstitute.org/sites/shanker/files/moneymatters_edition2.pdf on January 19, 2018.

Banathy, B. H. (1991). *Systems design of education: A journey to create the future.* Englewood Cliffs, NJ: Educational Technology.

Banathy, B. H. (1992). *A systems view of education: Concepts and principles for effective practice.* Englewood Cliffs, NJ: Educational Technology.

Bandura, A. (1977). Self-efficacy: Toward a unifying theory of behavioral change. *Psychological Review, 84*(2), 191–215.

Bandura, A. (1993). Perceived self-efficacy in cognitive development and functioning. *Educational Psychologist, 28*(2), 117–148.

Bandura, A. (1997). *Self-efficacy: The exercise of control.* New York: Freeman.

Barber, B. K., & Olsen, J. A. (2004). Assessing the transitions to middle and high school. *Journal of Adolescent Research, 19*(1), 3–30.

Barlow, V. E. (2001). *Trust and the principalship* (Unpublished manuscript). University of Calgary, Alberta, Canada. Accessed at www.ucalgary.ca/~cll/resources/trustandtheprincipalship.pdf on April 3, 2018.

Barth, R. S. (1990). *Improving schools from within: Teachers, parents, and principals can make the difference.* San Francisco: Jossey-Bass.

Bass, B. M. (1985). *Leadership and performance beyond expectations.* New York: Free Press.

Bennis, W. G., & Nanus, B. (1985). *Leaders: The strategies for taking charge*. New York: Harper & Row.

Biddle, B. J., & Berliner, D. C. (2002). A research synthesis: Unequal school funding in the United States. *Educational Leadership*, *59*(8), 48–59.

Blase, J., & Blase, J. (2001). *Empowering teachers: What successful principals do* (2nd ed.). Thousand Oaks, CA: Corwin Press.

Blase, J., Blase, J., Anderson, G. L., & Dungan, S. (1995). *Democratic principals in action: Eight pioneers*. Thousand Oaks, CA: Corwin Press.

Bloom, B. S. (1971). Mastery learning. In J. H. Block (Ed.), *Mastery learning: Theory and practice* (pp. 47–63). New York: Holt, Rinehart and Winston.

Bloom, B. S. (1977). Favorable learning conditions for all. *Teacher*, *95*(3), 22–28.

Boser, U., Wilhelm, M., & Hanna, R. (2014, October 6). *The power of the Pygmalion effect: Teachers' expectations strongly predict college completion*. Washington, DC: Center for American Progress. Accessed at www.americanprogress.org/issues/education-k-12/reports/2014/10/06/96806/the-power-of-the-pygmalion-effect on January 19, 2018.

Bramante, F., & Colby, R. (2012). *Off the clock: Moving education from time to competency*. Thousand Oaks, CA: Corwin Press.

Brookhart, S. M. (2008). *How to give effective feedback to your students*. Alexandria, VA: Association for Supervision and Curriculum Development.

Brown, B. (2012). *Daring greatly: How the courage to be vulnerable transforms the way we live, love, parent, and lead*. New York: Gotham Books.

Brown, B. (2015). *Rising strong: How the ability to reset transforms the way we live, love, parent, and lead*. New York: Random House.

Bryk, A. S., Sebring, P. B., Allensworth, E., Luppescu, S., & Easton, J. Q. (2010). *Organizing schools for improvement: Lessons from Chicago*. Chicago: University of Chicago Press.

Buffum, A., Mattos, M., & Weber, C. (2009). *Pyramid response to intervention: RTI, professional learning communities, and how to respond when kids don't learn*. Bloomington, IN: Solution Tree Press.

Burke, W. W. (2011). *Organization change: Theory and practice* (3rd ed.). Los Angeles: SAGE.

Burks, J., & Hochbein, C. (2013). The students in front of us: Reform for the current generation of urban high school students. *Urban Education*, *50*(3), 1–31, 346–376.

Burns, J. M. (1978). *Leadership*. New York: Harper & Row.

Busteed, B. (2013, January 7). *The school cliff: Student engagement drops with each school year* [Blog post]. Accessed at http://news.gallup.com/opinion/gallup/170525/school-cliff-student-engagement-drops-school-year.aspx on January 18, 2018.

Christenson, S. L., Reschly, A. L., & Wylie, C. (Eds.). (2012). *Handbook of research on student engagement.* New York: Springer.

Clynes, T. (2016). How to raise a genius: Lessons from a 45-year study of super-smart children. *Nature*, *537*(7619), 152–155.

Cohen, S., & Janicki-Deverts, D. (2012). Who's stressed? Distributions of psychological stress in the United States in probability samples from 1983, 2006, and 2009. *Journal of Applied Social Psychology*, *42*(6), 1320–1334.

Cook-Sather, A. (2002a). Authorizing students' perspectives: Toward trust, dialogue, and change in education. *Educational Researcher*, *31*(4), 3–14.

Cook-Sather, A. (2002b). Change based on what students say: Preparing teachers for a paradoxical model of leadership. *International Journal of Leadership in Education*, *9*(4), 345–358.

Cook-Sather, A. (2002c). Re(in)forming the conversations: Student position, power, and voice in teacher education. *The Radical Teacher*, *64*, 21–28.

Corbetta, M., & Shulman, G. L. (2002). Control of goal-directed and stimulus-driven attention in the brain. *Nature Reviews Neuroscience*, *3*(3), 201–215.

Cox, J. (2007). *Finding the story behind the numbers: A tool-based guide for evaluating educational programs.* Thousand Oaks, CA: Corwin Press.

Creswell, J. (2003). *Research design: Qualitative, quantitative, and mixed methods approaches* (2nd ed.). Thousand Oaks, CA: SAGE.

Csikszentmihalyi, M. (1990). *Flow: The psychology of optimal experience.* New York: Harper & Row.

Daggett, W. R., & McNulty, R. J. (2010). *Introducing Fred Bramante: Designer of fundamental change in the New Hampshire school system*. Rexford, NY: International Center for Leadership in Education.

Darling-Hammond, L. (2000). Teacher quality and student achievement: A review of state policy evidence. *Education Policy Analysis Archives*, *8*(1). Accessed at https://epaa.asu.edu/ojs/article/view/392/515 on February 8, 2018.

De Broucker, P. (2005). *Without a paddle: What to do about Canada's young drop-outs*. Ottawa, Canada: Canadian Policy Research Networks.

DeLorenzo, R. A., Battino, W. J., Schreiber, R. M., & Carrio, B. G. (2009). *Delivering on the promise: The education revolution*. Bloomington, IN: Solution Tree Press.

Dewey, J. (1899). *The school and society*. Chicago: University of Chicago Press.

Dewey, J. (1916). *Democracy and education: An introduction to the philosophy of education*. New York: Macmillan.

Dewey, J. (1938). *Experience and education*. New York: Macmillan.

De Wit, D. J., Karioja, K., & Rye, B. J. (2010). Student perceptions of diminished teacher and classmate support following the transition to high school: Are they related to declining attendance? *School Effectiveness and School Improvement*, *21*(4), 451–472.

DeWitt, P. (2017). Do leaders really understand the research they promote? *CorwinConnect*. Accessed at http://corwin-connect.com/2017/11/leaders-really-understand-research-promote on January 19, 2018.

DuFour, R., DuFour, R., & Eaker, R. (2008). *Revisiting Professional Learning Communities at Work: New insights for improving schools*. Bloomington, IN: Solution Tree Press.

DuFour, R., DuFour, R., Eaker, R., Many, T. W., & Mattos, M. (2016). *Learning by doing: A handbook for Professional Learning Communities at Work* (3rd ed.). Bloomington, IN: Solution Tree Press.

DuFour, R., & Eaker, R. (1998). *Professional Learning Communities at Work: Best practices for enhancing student achievement*. Bloomington, IN: Solution Tree Press.

Duncan, A. (2009). *A call to teaching: Secretary Arne Duncan's remarks at the rotunda at the University of Virginia* [Transcript]. Accessed at www.ed.gov/news/speeches/call-teaching on January 18, 2018.

Dweck, C. S. (1999). *Self-theories: Their role in motivation, personality, and development*. Philadelphia: Psychology Press.

Dweck, C. S. (2006). *Mindset: The new psychology of success*. New York: Random House.

Education Alliance. (2004). *A summary of research on using student voice in school improvement planning*. Accessed at http://docplayer.net/47266707-A-summary-of-research-on-using-student-voice-in-school-improvement-planning-funding-provided-by-the-claude-worthington-benedum-foundation.html on June 6, 2018.

Ericson, D. P., & Ellett, F. S. (2002, July 2). The question of the student in educational reform. *Education Policy Analysis Archives, 10*(31). Accessed at https://researchgate.net/profile/David_Ericson/publication/49610108_The_Question_of_the_Student_In_Educational_Reform/links/0deec51fc44522dd3f000000/The-Question-of-the-Student-In-Educational-Reform.pdf on March 15, 2018.

Ferguson, R. F. (2002). *Ed-excel assessment of secondary school student culture, tabulations by school district and race/ethnicity*. Cambridge, MA: Wiener Center for Social Policy, J. F. Kennedy School of Government, Harvard University.

Ferguson, R. F. (2015). *The influence of teaching: Beyond standardized test scores—Engagement, mindsets, and agency*. Accessed at www.agi.harvard.edu/projects/TeachingandAgency.pdf on May 1, 2018.

Fine, M., & Burns, A. (2003). Class notes: Toward a critical psychology of class and schooling. *Journal of Social Issues, 59*(4), 841–860.

Finn, J. D., & Rock, D. A. (1997). Academic success among students at risk for school failure. *Journal of Applied Psychology, 82*(2), 221–234.

Fredricks, J. A., Blumenfeld, P. C., & Paris, A. H. (2004). School engagement: Potential of the concept, state of the evidence. *Review of Educational Research, 74*(1), 59–109.

Fredricks, J. A., McColskey, W., Meli, J., Mordica, J., Montrosse, B., & Mooney, K. (2011). *Measuring student engagement in upper elementary through high school: A description of 21 instruments*. Greensboro, NC: REL Southeast.

Freire, P. (1970). *Pedagogy of the oppressed*. New York: Herder and Herder.

Frey, C. B., & Osborne, M. A. (2013). *The future of employment: How susceptible are jobs to computerisation?* Accessed at www.oxfordmartin.ox.ac.uk/downloads/academic/The_Future_of_Employment.pdf on May 29, 2018.

Friedman, T. L. (2016). *Thank you for being late: An optimist's guide to thriving in the age of accelerations.* New York: Farrar, Straus & Giroux.

Fullan, M. (2001). *Leading in a culture of change.* San Francisco: Jossey-Bass.

Fullan, M. (2003). *The moral imperative of school leadership.* Thousand Oaks, CA: Corwin Press.

Fullan, M. (2007). *The new meaning of educational change* (4th ed.). New York: Teachers College Press.

Fullan, M. (2008). *The six secrets of change: What the best leaders do to help their organizations survive and thrive.* San Francisco: Jossey-Bass.

Fullan, M. (2010). *All systems go: The change imperative for whole system reform.* Thousand Oaks, CA: Corwin Press.

Fullan, M. (2011). *Change leader: Learning to do what matters most.* San Francisco: Jossey-Bass.

Fullan, M., & Miles, M. B. (1992). Getting reform right: What works and what doesn't. *Phi Delta Kappan, 73,* 745–752.

Furrer, C., & Skinner, E. (2003). Sense of relatedness as a factor in children's academic engagement and performance. *Journal of Educational Psychology, 95*(1), 148–162.

Gardner, H. (1993). *Multiple intelligences: The theory in practice.* New York: Basic Books.

Gehlbach, H., & Brinkworth, M. E. (2011). Measure twice, cut down error: A process for enhancing the validity of survey scales. *Review of General Psychology, 15*(4), 380–387.

Geijsel, F. P., Sleegers, P. J. C., Stoel, R. D., & Krüger, M. L. (2009). The effect of teacher psychological, school organizational and leadership factors on teachers' professional learning in Dutch schools. *Elementary School Journal, 109*(4), 406–427.

General Electric Company. (2001). *GE annual report 2000.* Accessed at www.ge.com/annual00/download/images/GEannual00.pdf on January 18, 2018.

Gettinger, M., & Ball, C. (2007). Best practices in increasing academic engaged time. In A. Thomas & J. Grimes (Eds.), *Best practices in school psychology* (vol. V, pp. 1043–1075). Bethesda, MD: National Association of School Psychologists.

Gewertz, C. (2003). N.Y.C. chancellor aims to bolster instructional leadership. *Education Week, 22*(16), 7, 12.

Gleason, S. C., & Gerzon, N. (2013). *Growing into equity: Professional learning and personalization in high-achieving schools.* Thousand Oaks, CA: Corwin Press.

Goddard, R. D. (2001). Collective efficacy: A neglected construct in the study of schools and student achievement. *Journal of Educational Psychology, 93*(3), 467–476.

Goddard, R. D., Hoy, W. K., & Hoy, A. W. (2000). Collective teacher efficacy: Its meaning, measure, and impact on student achievement. *American Educational Research Journal, 37*(2), 479–507.

Goddard, R. D., Hoy, W. K., & Hoy, A. W. (2004). Collective efficacy beliefs: Theoretical developments, empirical evidence, and future directions. *Educational Researcher, 33*(3), 3–13.

Goddard, R. D., Sweetland, S. R., & Hoy, W. K. (2000). Academic emphasis of urban elementary schools and student achievement in reading and mathematics: A multilevel analysis. *Educational Administration Quarterly, 36*(5), 683–702.

Goddard, R. D., Tschannen-Moran, M., & Hoy, W. K. (2001). A multilevel examination of the distribution and effects of teacher trust in students and parents in urban elementary schools. *Elementary School Journal, 102*(1), 3–17.

Graetz, G., & Michaels, G. (2015). *Robots at work* (CEP Discussion Paper No. 1335). London: Centre for Economic Performance, London School of Economics and Political Science. Accessed at http://cep.lse.ac.uk/pubs/download/dp1335.pdf on May 29, 2018.

Greenleaf, R. K. (1977). *Servant leadership: A journey into the nature of legitimate power and greatness.* New York: Paulist Press.

Guskey, T. R. (1997). *Implementing mastery learning* (2nd ed.). Belmont, CA: Wadsworth.

Guskey, T. R. (2007). Closing achievement gaps: Revisiting Benjamin S. Bloom's "Learning for Mastery." *Journal of Advanced Academics, 19*(1), 8–31.

Guskey, T. R. (2008). Mastery learning. In T. L. Good (Ed.), *21st century education: A reference handbook* (vol. 1, pp. 194–202). Thousand Oaks, CA: SAGE.

Guskey, T. R. (2010). Lessons of mastery learning. *Educational Leadership, 68*(2), 52–57.

Hall, G. E., & Hord, S. M. (2011). *Implementing change: Patterns, principles, and potholes* (3rd ed.). Upper Saddle River, NJ: Pearson Education.

Hallinger, P. (2012). *School leadership that makes a difference: Lessons from 30 years of international research.* Accessed at www.utsbasilicata.it/attachments/article/810/03a_Leadership_21st_century_schools[1].pdf on January 19, 2018.

Hallinger, P., & Murphy, J. (1985). Assessing the instructional leadership behavior of principals. *Elementary School Journal, 86*(2), 217–248.

Harris, D. (2014). *10% happier: How I tamed the voice in my head, reduced stress without losing my edge, and found self-help that actually works—A true story*. New York: HarperCollins.

Hattie, J. (2009). *Visible learning: A synthesis of over 800 meta-analyses relating to achievement.* New York: Routledge.

Hattie, J. (2012). *Visible learning for teachers: Maximizing impact on learning.* London: Routledge.

Hattie, J. (2015). High-impact leadership. *Educational Leadership, 72*(5), 36–40.

Heckman, J. J. (2011). The economics of inequality: The value of early childhood education. *American Educator, 35*(1), 31–47.

Heflebower, T., Hoegh, J. K., & Warrick, P. (2014). *A school leader's guide to standards-based grading.* Bloomington, IN: Marzano Resources.

Heifetz, R. A., & Linsky, M. (2002). *Leadership on the line: Staying alive through the dangers of leading.* Boston: Harvard Business School Press.

Hellriegel, D., & Slocum, J. W. (2009). *Organizational behavior* (12th ed.). Mason, OH: Cengage Learning.

Howard, T. C. (2001). Telling their side of the story: African-American students' perceptions of culturally relevant teaching. *The Urban Review, 33*(2), 131–149.

Howard, T. C. (2002). Hearing footsteps in the dark: African-American students' descriptions of effective teachers. *Journal of Education for Students Placed at Risk, 7*(4), 425–444.

Hoy, W. K. (2002). Faculty trust: A key to student achievement. *Journal of School Public Relations, 23*(2), 88–103.

Hoy, W. K. (2005). *SAOS*. Accessed at http://waynekhoy.com/pdfs/saos.pdf on March 2, 2018.

Hoy, W. K. (2015). *Academic optimism of schools*. Accessed at http://waynekhoy.com/collective-ao.html on March 2, 2018.

Hoy, W. K., & Miskel, C. G. (2005). *Educational administration: Theory, research, and practice* (7th ed.). New York: McGraw-Hill.

Hoy, W. K., Tarter, C. J., & Hoy, A. W. (2006a). Academic optimism of schools: A force for student achievement. *American Educational Research Journal, 43*(3), 425–446.

Hoy, W. K., Tarter, C. J., & Hoy, A. W. (2006b). Academic optimism of schools: A second-order confirmatory factor analysis. In W. K. Hoy & C. Miskel (Eds.), *Contemporary issues in educational policy and school outcomes* (pp. 135–157). Greenwich, CT: Information Age.

Hyacinth, B. (2017, November 15). *Why employees come first, customers second, and shareholders third* [Blog post]. Accessed at www.linkedin.com/pulse/why-employees-come-first-customers-second-third-brigette-hyacinth on January 19, 2018.

Iacoboni, M. (2009). *Mirroring people: The science of empathy and how we connect with others*. New York: Picador.

Iberlin, J. M. (2017). *Cultivating mindfulness in the classroom*. Bloomington, IN: Marzano Resources.

Ingersoll, R., & May, H. (2016). *Minority teacher recruitment, employment, and retention: 1987 to 2013* (Issue brief). Palo Alto, CA: Learning Policy Institute.

Ingersoll, R., Merrill, L., & May, H. (2016a). Do accountability policies push teachers out? *Educational Leadership, 73*(8), 44–49.

Ingersoll, R., Merrill, L., & May, H. (2016b). *What are the effects of school accountability on teacher turnover?* (CPRE research report). Philadelphia: Consortium for Policy Research in Education, University of Pennsylvania.

Jensen, E. (2008). *Brain-based learning: The new paradigm of teaching* (2nd ed.). Thousand Oaks, CA: Corwin Press.

Jerald, C. D., & Ingersoll, R. (2002). *All talk no action: Putting an end to out-of-field teaching*. Accessed at https://repository.upenn.edu/gse_pubs/142 on January 19, 2018.

Kabat-Zinn, J. (2005). *Wherever you go, there you are: Mindfulness meditation in everyday life*. New York: Hyperion.

Kanevsky, L., & Keighley, T. (2003). To produce or not to produce? Understanding boredom and the honor in underachievement. *Roeper Review, 26*(1), 20–28.

Kaplan, J. (2015). *Humans need not apply: A guide to wealth and work in the age of artificial intelligence.* New Haven, CT: Yale University Press.

Katayama, D. (2012, June 12). *Studies favor JCPS turnaround model "Project Proficiency."* Accessed at https://wfpl.org/studies-favor-jcps-turnaround-model-project-proficiency on July 16, 2018.

Kena, G., Aud, S., Johnson, F., Wang, X., Zhang, J., Rathbun, A., et al. (2014). *The condition of education 2014* (NCES 2014–083). Washington, DC: U.S. Department of Education, National Center for Education Statistics. Accessed at https://nces.ed.gov/pubs2014/2014083.pdf on January 31, 2018.

Kennedy, M. M. (2005). *Inside teaching: How classroom life undermines reform.* Cambridge, MA: Harvard University Press.

Khadaroo, S. T. (2013). Is your student "competent"? A new education yardstick takes the measure. *Christian Science Monitor.* Accessed at www.csmonitor.com/USA/Education/2013/0814/Is-your-student-competent-A-new-education-yardstick-takes-the-measure on January 19, 2018.

King, M. L. Jr. (2010). *Stride toward freedom: The Montgomery story.* Boston: Beacon Press.

Kohn, A. (1993). *Punished by rewards: The trouble with gold stars, incentive plans, A's, praise, and other bribes.* Boston: Houghton Mifflin.

Kohn, A. (1999). *The schools our children deserve: Moving beyond traditional classrooms and "tougher standards."* Boston: Houghton Mifflin.

Krüger, M. L., Witziers, B., & Sleegers, P. (2007). The impact of school leadership on school level factors: Validation of a causal model. *School Effectiveness and School Improvement, 18*(1), 1–20.

Kübler-Ross, E. (1969). *On death and dying: What the dying have to teach doctors, nurses, clergy, and their own families.* New York: Macmillan.

Kuhn, T. S. (1970). *The structure of scientific revolutions* (2nd ed.). Chicago: University of Chicago Press.

Kulik, C-L. C., Kulik, J. A., & Bangert-Drowns, R. L. (1990). Effectiveness of mastery learning programs: A meta-analysis. *Review of Educational Research, 60*(2), 265–299.

Kyriacou, C. (1987). Teacher stress and burnout: An international review. *Educational Research, 29*(2), 146–152.

Larson, R., & Barton, R. (2013). Lessons on leading for equity. *Principal Leadership, 13*(8), 18–24.

Leithwood, K. A. (1992). The move toward transformational leadership. *Educational Leadership, 49*(5), 8–12.

Leithwood, K. A., & Jantzi, D. (2006). Transformational school leadership for large-scale reform: Effects on students, teachers, and their classroom practices. *School Effectiveness and School Improvement, 17*(2), 201–227.

Leithwood, K. A., Jantzi, D., & Steinbach, R. (1999). *Changing leadership for changing times*. Buckingham, England: Open University Press.

Levin, B. (2000). Putting students at the centre in education reform. *Journal of Educational Change, 1*(2), 155–172.

Lindsay Unified School District. (2017). *Beyond reform: Systemic shifts toward personalized learning*. Bloomington, IN: Marzano Resources.

Linn, R. L. (2001). A century of standardized testing: Controversies and pendulum swings. *Educational Assessment, 7*(1), 29–38.

Littky, D. (2004). *The big picture: Education is everyone's business*. Alexandria, VA: Association for Supervision and Curriculum Development.

Lubinski, D., Benbow, C. P., & Kell, H. J. (2014). Life paths and accomplishments of mathematically precocious males and females four decades later. *Psychological Science, 25*(12), 2217–2232.

Mandela, N. (2003). *Lighting your way to a better future: Speech delivered by Mr. N. R. Mandela at launch of Mindset Network* [Transcript]. Accessed at http://db.nelsonmandela.org/speeches/pub_view.asp?pg=item&ItemID=NMS909&txtstr=education%20is%20the%20most%20powerful on January 18, 2018.

Marks, H. (2000). Student engagement in instructional activity: Patterns in the elementary, middle, and high school years. *American Educational Research Journal, 37*(1), 153–184.

Marsh, H., & Craven, R. (2006). Reciprocal effects of self-concept and performance from a multidimensional perspective: Beyond seductive pleasure and unidimensional perspectives. *Perspectives on Psychological Science, 1*(2), 133–163.

Marsh, H., & O'Mara, A. (2008). Reciprocal effects between academic self-concept, self-esteem, achievement, and attainment over seven adolescent years: Unidimensional and multidimensional perspectives of self-concept. *Personality and Social Psychology Bulletin, 34*(4), 542–552.

Martin, A. J. (2006). Personal bests (PBs): A proposed multidimensional model and empirical analysis. *British Journal of Educational Psychology, 76*(4), 803–825.

Martin, A. J. (2011). Personal best (PB) approaches to academic development: Implications for motivation and assessment. *Educational Practice and Theory, 33*(1), 93–99.

Martin, A. J. (2012a). *The motivation and engagement workbook* (12th ed.). Sydney, Australia: Lifelong Achievement Group.

Martin, A. J. (2012b). The role of personal best (PB) goals in the achievement and behavioral engagement of students with ADHD and students without ADHD. *Contemporary Educational Psychology, 37*(2), 91–105.

Martin, A. J., & Liem, G. A. D. (2010). Academic personal bests (PBs), engagement, and achievement: A cross-lagged panel analysis. *Learning and Individual Differences, 20*(3), 265–270.

Marzano, R. J. (2003). *What works in schools: Translating research into action.* Alexandria, VA: Association for Supervision and Curriculum Development.

Marzano, R. J. (2007). *The art and science of teaching: A comprehensive framework for effective instruction.* Alexandria, VA: Association for Supervision and Curriculum Development.

Marzano, R. J. (2010). *Formative assessment and standards-based grading.* Bloomington, IN: Marzano Resources.

Marzano, R. J. (2012). *Becoming a reflective teacher.* Bloomington, IN: Marzano Resources.

Marzano, R. J. (2017). *The new art and science of teaching.* Bloomington, IN: Solution Tree Press.

Marzano, R. J. (2018). *Making classroom assessments reliable and valid.* Bloomington, IN: Solution Tree Press.

Marzano, R. J., Frontier, T., & Livingston, D. (2011). *Effective supervision: Supporting the art and science of teaching.* Alexandria, VA: Association for Supervision and Curriculum Development.

Marzano, R. J., Heflebower, T., Hoegh, J. K., Warrick, P., & Grift, G. (2016). *Collaborative teams that transform schools: The next step in PLCs*. Bloomington, IN: Marzano Resources.

Marzano, R. J., & Marzano, J. S. (2015). *Managing the inner world of teaching: Emotions, interpretations, and actions*. Bloomington, IN: Marzano Resources.

Marzano, R. J., Norford, J. S., Finn, M., & Finn, D., III. (2017). *A handbook for personalized competency-based education*. Bloomington, IN: Marzano Resources.

Marzano, R. J., Warrick, P., & Simms, J. A. (2014). *A handbook for high reliability schools: The next step in school reform*. Bloomington, IN: Marzano Resources.

Marzano, R. J., Waters, T., & McNulty, B. A. (2005). *School leadership that works: From research to results*. Alexandria, VA: Association for Supervision and Curriculum Development.

Marzano, R. J., Yanoski, D. C., Hoegh, J. K., & Simms, J. A. (2013). *Using Common Core standards to enhance classroom instruction and assessment*. Bloomington, IN: Marzano Resources.

McFarland, J., Hussar, B., de Brey, C., Snyder, T., Wang, X., Wilkinson-Flicker, S., et al. (2017). *The condition of education 2017* (NCES 2017–144). Washington, DC: U.S. Department of Education, National Center for Education Statistics. Accessed at https://nces.ed.gov/pubsearch/pubsinfo.asp?pubid=2017144 on January 19, 2018.

McGuigan, L., & Hoy, W. K. (2006). Principal leadership: Creating a culture of academic optimism to improve achievement for all students. *Leadership and Policy in Schools*, *5*(3), 203–229.

Meltzer, L. (Ed.). (2010). *Executive function in education: From theory to practice*. New York: Guilford Press.

Mesa County Valley School District 51. (2018). *D51 learning model*. Accessed at www.d51schools.org/about_us/performance_based_learning on June 4, 2018.

MetLife. (2013). *The MetLife survey of the American teacher: Challenges for school leadership*. New York: Author.

Metropolitan Regional Career and Technical Center (2017). *Student success*. Accessed at www.themethighschool.org/apps/pages/index.jsp?uREC_ID=376959&type=d&pREC_ID=852613 on January 23, 2018.

Michigan Department of Education. (2017). *Standard teaching certificate renewal.* Accessed at www.michigan.gov/documents/mde/ProvCertRenewal_530866_7.pdf on June 12, 2018.

Mintz, S., & McNeil, S. (2016). The struggle for public schools. *Digital History.* Accessed at www.digitalhistory.uh.edu/disp_textbook.cfm?smtID=2&psid=3535 on June 12, 2018.

Missouri Department of Elementary & Secondary Education. (n.d.). *Required professional development hours.* Accessed at https://dese.mo.gov/educator-quality/certification/required-professional-development-hours on June 12, 2018.

Mitra, D. (2006). Increasing student voice and moving toward youth leadership. *Prevention Researcher, 13*(1), 7–10.

Moolenaar, N. M., Daly, A. J., & Sleegers, P. J. C. (2010). Occupying the principal position: Examining relationships between transformational leadership, social network position, and schools' innovative climate. *Educational Administration Quarterly, 46*(5), 623–670.

Muhammad, A. (2009). *Transforming school culture: How to overcome staff division.* Bloomington, IN: Solution Tree Press.

Muhammad, A. (2018). *Transforming school culture: How to overcome staff division* (2nd ed.). Bloomington, IN: Solution Tree Press.

National Commission on Excellence in Education. (1983). *A nation at risk.* Washington, DC: Author. Accessed at https://www2.ed.gov/pubs/NatAtRisk/risk.html on February 20, 2018.

National Education Commission on Time and Learning. (2000). *Prisoners of time: Too much to teach, not enough time to teach it.* Peterborough, NH: Crystal Springs Books.

National Institute of Mental Health. (2016). *Anxiety disorders.* Accessed at www.nimh.nih.gov/health/topics/anxiety-disorders/index.shtml on June 4, 2018.

National Institutes of Health. (2012, August 28). *Stresses of poverty may impair learning ability in young children* [Press release]. Accessed at www.nih.gov/news-events/news-releases/stresses-poverty-may-impair-learning-ability-young-children on January 18, 2018.

National Research Council & Institute of Medicine. (2004). *Engaging schools: Fostering high school students' motivation to learn*. Washington, DC: National Academies Press.

Noguera, P. A. (2003). *City schools and the American dream*. New York: Teachers College Press.

Northouse, P. G. (2007). *Leadership: Theory and practice* (4th ed.). Thousand Oaks, CA: SAGE.

Nuthall, G. (2001, December). *The cultural myths and the realities of teaching and learning*. Unpublished Jean Herbison lecture, University of Canterbury. Accessed at www.educationalleaders.govt.nz/content/download/482/3676/Graham_Nuthall_2001.pdf on March 1, 2018.

Nuthall, G. (2002). The cultural myths and the realities of teaching and learning. *New Zealand Annual Review of Education, 11*, 5–30.

Organisation for Economic Co-operation and Development. (2017). United States. In *Education at a glance 2017: OECD indicators*. Paris: Author. Accessed at www.keepeek.com/Digital-Asset-Management/embed-oecd/education/education-at-a-glance-2017/united-states_eag-2017-72-en#.Wi11xlQ-eT9 on January 23, 2018.

Osberg, J., Pope, D., & Galloway, M. (2006). Students matter in school reform: Leaving fingerprints and becoming leaders. *International Journal of Leadership in Education, 9*(4), 329–343.

Palmer, P. J. (2007). A new professional: The aims of education revisited. *Change: The Magazine of Higher Learning, 39*(6), 6–12.

Panorama Education. (2015). *User guide: Panorama student survey*. Accessed at https://panorama-www.s3.amazonaws.com/files/panorama-student-survey/User-Guide.pdf?__hssc=17850406.1.1520026169024&__hstc=17850406.6a66d65e9beb132860d9946c6537b454.1520003118080.1520003118080.1520026169024.2&__hsfp=4030342268&hsCtaTracking=ef4fd9f4-f6c2-474a-9d37-0a95a80b09ae%7C36a69aba-bb58-4f6a-addf-89c106ad7b85 on March 2, 2018.

Peterson, C. (2000). The future of optimism. *American Psychologist, 55*(1), 44–55.

Pink, D. H. (2005). *A whole new mind: Moving from the information age to the conceptual age*. New York: Riverhead Books.

Pink, D. H. (2009). *Drive: The surprising truth about what motivates us*. New York: Riverhead Books.

Pintrich, P. R. (2003). A motivational science perspective on the role of student motivation in learning and teaching contexts. *Journal of Educational Psychology, 95*(4), 667–686.

Plemmons, G., Hall, M., Doupnik, S., Gay, J., Brown, C., Browning, W., Casey, R., Freundlich, K., Johnson, D. P., Lind, C., Rehm, K., Thomas, S., & Williams, D. (2018). Hospitalization for suicide ideation or attempt: 2008–2015. *Pediatrics, 141*(6).

Priest, N., Rudenstine, A., Weisstein, E., & Gerwin, C. (2012). *Making mastery work: A close-up view of competency education*. Quincy, MA: Nellie Mae Education Foundation.

Quaglia Institute for Student Aspirations. (2012). *My voice national student report, grades 6–12*. Portland, ME: Author. Accessed at www.quagliainstitute.org/dmsView/2012_NationalReport_FINAL on March 16, 2018.

Quaglia Institute for Student Aspirations. (2014). *My voice national student report, grades 6–12: A QISA Aspirations Research Center study*. Portland, ME: Author. Accessed at www.quagliainstitute.org/dmsView/My_Voice_2013-2014_National_Report_8_25 on January 23, 2018.

Quaglia, R. J., & Cobb, C. D. (1996). Toward a theory of student aspirations. *Journal of Research in Rural Education, 12*(3), 127–132.

Ratcliffe, C., & McKernan, S.-M. (2012). *Child poverty and its lasting consequence*. Accessed at www.urban.org/research/publication/child-poverty-and-its-lasting-consequence on January 23, 2018.

Ravitch, D. (2000). *Left back: A century of battles over school reform*. New York: Simon & Schuster.

Raymond, L. (2001). Student involvement in school improvement: From data source to significant voice. *FORUM, 43*(2), 58–61.

Reeves, D. B. (n.d.). Leave me alone and let me teach! [Blog post]. *American Association of School Administrators*. Accessed at www.aasa.org/SchoolAdministratorArticle.aspx?id=10646 on June 4, 2018.

Reeves, D. B. (2002). *Holistic accountability: Serving students, schools, and community*. Thousand Oaks, CA: Corwin Press.

Renzulli, J. S. (1978). What makes giftedness? Reexamining a definition. *Phi Delta Kappan, 60*(3), 180–184, 261.

Renzulli, J. S. (2008). Engagement is the answer. *Education Week, 27*(43), 30–31.

Reschly, A. L., Huebner, E. S., Appleton, J. J., & Antaramian, S. (2008). Engagement as flourishing: The contribution of positive emotions and coping to adolescents' engagement at school and with learning. *Psychology in the Schools, 45*(5), 419–431.

Reyes, M. R., Brackett, M. A., Rivers, S. E., White, M., & Salovey, P. (2012). Classroom emotional climate, student engagement, and academic achievement. *Journal of Educational Psychology, 104*(3), 700–712. Accessed at https://pdfs.semanticscholar.org/3e7e/ee534bfbd680898064f866cbb678a51f30d5.pdf on May 9, 2018.

Richmond, E. (2013). Teacher job satisfaction hits 25-year low. *The Atlantic.* Accessed at www.theatlantic.com/national/archive/2013/02/teacher-job-satisfaction-hits-25-year-low/273383 on May 29, 2018.

Rizzolatti, G., & Sinigaglia, C. (2008). *Mirrors in the brain: How our minds share actions and emotions.* New York: Oxford University Press.

Robinson, K. (2001). *Out of our minds: Learning to be creative.* West Sussex, England: Capstone.

Robinson, K. (2013, May 3). *Why we need to reform education now* [Blog post]. Accessed at https://huffingtonpost.com/sir-ken-robinson/reform-american-education-now_b_3203949.html on May 16, 2018.

Robinson, V. M. J., Lloyd, C. A., & Rowe, K. J. (2008). The impact of leadership on student outcomes: An analysis of the differential effects of leadership types. *Educational Administration Quarterly, 44*(5), 635–674.

The Ron Clark Academy. (2018). *Who we are.* Accessed at www.ronclarkacademy.com on June 4, 2018.

Ross, A. (2016). *The industries of the future.* New York: Simon & Schuster.

Rubinson, F. (2004). Urban dropouts: Why so many and what can be done? In S. Steinberg & J. Kincheloe (Eds.), *19 urban questions: Teaching in the city* (pp. 53–67). New York: Lang.

Rumberger, R. W., & Lim, S. A. (2008). *Why students drop out of school: A review of 25 years of research* (California Dropout Research Project report #15). Accessed at https://issuelab.org/resources/11658/11658.pdf on January 19, 2018.

Ruyle, M. A. (2014). *Student engagement, academic optimism, and leadership: A case study of performance-based schools* (Doctoral dissertation). Montana State University, Bozeman. Accessed at https://pqdtopen.proquest.com/doc/1660528409.html?FMT=AI on January 18, 2018.

Ryan, R. M., & Deci, E. L. (2000). Intrinsic and extrinsic motivations: Classic definitions and new directions. *Contemporary Educational Psychology, 25*(1), 54–67.

Sanders, W. L., & Rivers, J. C. (1996). *Cumulative and residual effects of teachers on future student academic achievement* [Research progress report]. Knoxville, TN: University of Tennessee Value-Added Research and Assessment Center.

Sands, D. I., Guzman, L., Stephens, L., & Boggs, A. (2007). Including student voices in school reform: Students speak out. *Journal of Latinos and Education, 6*(4), 323–345.

Sandstrom, H., & Huerta, S. (2013). The negative effects of instability on child development. *Urban Institute*. Accessed at https://www.urban.org/sites/default/files/publication/32721/412908-The-Negative-Effects-of-Instability-on-Child-Development-Fact-Sheet.PDF on January 23, 2018.

Schenck, J. (2011). *Teaching and the adolescent brain: An educator's guide*. New York: Norton.

Schlechty, P. C. (2002). *Working on the work: An action plan for teachers, principals, and superintendents*. San Francisco: Jossey-Bass.

Schmoker, M. (2006). *Results now*. Alexandria, VA: Association for Supervision and Curriculum Development.

Schontzler, G. (2012, June 2). Bridger Alternative: Making miracles possible for students in trouble. *Bozeman Daily Chronicle*. Accessed at https://bozemandailychronicle.com/news/education/bridger-alternative-making-miracles-possible-for-students-in-trouble/article_dd8d8b1a-ac64-11e1-b46f-0019bb2963f4.html on February 8, 2018.

Schrobsdorff, S. (2016, October 27). Teen depression and anxiety: Why the kids are not alright. *Time.* Accessed at www.time.com/magazine/us/4547305/november-7th-2016-vol-188-no-19-u-s on January 23, 2018.

Schunk, D. H. (2012). *Learning theories: An educational perspective* (6th ed.). Boston: Pearson.

Schwahn, C., & McGarvey, B. (2012). *Inevitable: Mass customized learning, learning in the age of empowerment.* Lexington, KY: CreateSpace.

Schwahn, C., & McGarvey, B. (2014). *Inevitable too!: The total leader embraces mass customized learning.* Lexington, KY: CreateSpace.

Sebring, P. B., & Bryk, A. S. (2000). School leadership and the bottom line in Chicago. *Phi Delta Kappan, 81*(6), 440–443.

Segal, C. (2014, October 7). Teachers expect less from black and Hispanic students, study shows. *PBS NewsHour.* Accessed at www.pbs.org/newshour/nation/teachers-expect-less-students-color-study-shows on January 23, 2018.

Semrud-Clikeman, M. (2007). *Social competence in children and adolescents.* New York: Springer.

Sergiovanni, T. J. (1992). *Moral leadership: Getting to the heart of school improvement.* San Francisco: Jossey-Bass.

Simon, N. S., & Johnson, S. M. (2013). *Teacher turnover in high-poverty schools: What we know and can do* [Working paper]. Accessed at https://pdfs.semanticscholar.org/6210/6fb22387ad72a41d26403ec6851b2f0fd71c.pdf on May 29, 2018.

Sinar, E., Wellins, R., Paese, M., Smith, A., & Watt, B. (2016). *High-resolution leadership: A synthesis of 15,000 assessments into how leaders shape the business landscape.* Accessed at www.ddiworld.com/DDI/media/trend-research/high-resolution-leadership-2015-2016_tr_ddi.pdf?ext=.pdf on January 23, 2018.

Skaalvik, E. M., & Skaalvik, S. (2010). Teacher self-efficacy and teacher burnout: A study of relations. *Teaching and Teacher Education, 26*(4), 1059–1069. Accessed at www.researchgate.net/publication/222821947_Teacher_self-efficacy_and_teacher_burnout_A_study_of_relations_Teaching_and_Teacher_Education_264_1059-1069 on January 23, 2018.

Skinner, E., & Belmont, M. J. (1993). Motivation in the classroom: Reciprocal effects of teacher behavior and student engagement across the school year. *Journal of Educational Psychology, 85*(4), 571–581.

Skinner, E., Furrer, C., Marchand, G., & Kindermann, T. (2008). Engagement and disaffection in the classroom: Part of a larger motivational dynamic? *Journal of Educational Psychology, 100*(4), 765–781.

Smith, P. A., & Hoy, W. K. (2007). Academic optimism and student achievement in urban elementary schools. *Journal of Educational Administration, 45*(5), 556–568.

Smith, P. A., Hoy, W. K., & Sweetland, S. R. (2001). Organizational health of high schools and dimensions of faculty trust. *Journal of School Leadership, 11*, 135–151.

Smyth, J. (2006). "When students have power": Student engagement, student voice, and the possibilities for school reform around "dropping out" of school. *International Journal of Leadership in Education, 9*(4), 285–298.

Spencer, J. (2017). *Making learning flow*. Bloomington, IN: Solution Tree Press.

Stern, J. (1995). *The state of state education accountability* [Policy brief]. Charleston, WV: AEL.

Strauss, V. (2017, September 14). Teachers in U.S. paid far less than similarly educated professionals, report finds. *Washington Post*. Accessed at www.washingtonpost.com/news/answer-sheet/wp/2017/09/14/teachers-in-u-s-paid-nearly-60-percent-less-than-other-professionals-report-finds on January 23, 2018.

Strong, R., Silver, H. F., & Robinson, A. (1995). Strengthening student engagement: What do students want (and what really motivates them)? *Educational Leadership, 53*(1), 8–12.

Sturgis, C. (2016, February 15). *Lake County Schools: Designing a strategy to bring personalized learning to scale*. Accessed at http://competencyworks.org/case-study/lake-county-schools-designing-a-strategy-to-bring-personalized-learning-to-scale/ on January 2, 2017.

Sutcher, L., Darling-Hammond, L., & Carver-Thomas, D. (2016). *A coming crisis in teaching? Teacher supply, demand, and shortages in the U.S.* Palo Alto, CA: Learning Policy Institute.

Tavris, C., & Aronson, E. (2007). *Mistakes were made (but not by me): Why we justify foolish beliefs, bad decisions, and hurtful acts*. New York: Houghton Mifflin Harcourt.

Texas Education Agency. (n.d.). *Continuing professional education information.* Accessed at https://tea.texas.gov/Texas_Educators/Preparation_and_Continuing_Education/Continuing_Professional_Education_(CPE)/Continuing_Professional_Education_Information on June 12, 2018.

Timperley, H., Wilson, A., Barrar, H., & Fung, I. (2007). *Teacher professional learning and development: Best evidence synthesis iteration.* Wellington, New Zealand: Ministry of Education.

Turnbull, B. J., Riley, D. L., Arcaira, E. R., Anderson, L. M., & MacFarlane, J. R. (2013, July). *Six districts begin the principal pipeline initiative.* Accessed at www.wallacefoundation.org/knowledge-center/Documents/Six-Districts-Begin-the-Principal-Pipeline-Initiative.pdf on February 9, 2018.

Tyler, R. W. (1949). *Basic principles of curriculum and instruction.* Chicago: University of Chicago Press.

U.S. Department of Education. (n.d.). *Competency-based learning or personalized learning.* Accessed at www.ed.gov/oii-news/competency-based-learning-or-personalized-learning on June 1, 2018.

U.S. Department of Education. (2015, June). *Highly qualified teachers enrolled in programs providing alternative routes to teacher certification or licensure.* Washington, DC: Author. Accessed at www2.ed.gov/rschstat/eval/teaching/hqt-teacher-certification/report.pdf on January 18, 2018.

Vander Ark, T. (2015). *Smart cities need great schools: The best antidote to poverty.* Accessed at www.gettingsmart.com/2015/11/smart-cities-need-great-schools-the-best-antidote-to-poverty on January 23, 2018.

Virginia Department of Education. (2004). *Virginia drive to strengthen school leadership wins additional funding from the Wallace Foundation: Effective leadership is key to raising student achievement.* Accessed at www.doe.virginia.gov/VDOE/NewHome/pressreleases/2004/apr26.html on June 12, 2018.

Waters, T., & Cameron, G. (2007). *The balanced leadership framework: Connecting vision with action.* Denver, CO: McREL.

Waters, T., Marzano, R. J., & McNulty, B. (2003). *Balanced leadership: What 30 years of research tells us about the effect of leadership on student achievement.* Aurora, CO: Mid-Continent Research for Education and Learning. Accessed at www.mcrel.org/wp-content/uploads/2016/06/Balanced-Leadership%C2%AE-What-30-Years-of-Research-Tells-Us-about-the-Effect-of-Leadership-on-Student-Achievement.pdf on June 12, 2018.

Weisberg, D., Sexton, S., Mulhern, J., & Keeling, D. (2009). *The widget effect: Our national failure to acknowledge and act on differences in teacher effectiveness* (2nd ed.). New York: New Teacher Project.

Willink, J., & Babin, L. (2015). *Extreme ownership: How U.S. Navy SEALS lead and win.* New York: St. Martin's Press.

Wiser, M. (2013, March 24). New education theory in Iowa: Teach kids at their own pace. *Sioux City Journal.* Accessed at http://siouxcityjournal.com/news/local/education/new-education-theory-in-iowa-teach-kids-at-their-own/article_45b2a584-4984-5cd8-ae57-4a4a6576aac7.html on February 8, 2018.

Yazzie-Mintz, E. (2007). *Voices of students on engagement: A report on the 2006 high school survey of student engagement.* Bloomington, IN: Indiana University, Center for Evaluation and Education Policy. Accessed at https://files.eric.ed.gov/fulltext/ED495758.pdf on February 21, 2018.

Yazzie-Mintz, E. (2010). *Charting the path from engagement to achievement: A report on the 2009 high school survey of student engagement.* Bloomington: Indiana University, Center for Evaluation and Education Policy.

Yukl, G. (1989). Managerial leadership: A review of theory and research. *Journal of Management, 15*(2), 251–289.

INDEX

D

E

F

G

M

S

T

Parking Lot